CONTENTS

Published by SEO FREQUENCY

ACKNOWLEDGM ENTS

I would like to sincerely thank the individuals and organizations who have been instrumental in bringing this book to life. Their support, encouragement, and contributions have been invaluable:

- To my parents, for their unwavering love, support, and encouragement throughout my life and this writing journey.

- I extend my heartfelt gratitude to my wife, whose patience, understanding, and unwavering belief in my work made it possible for me to dedicate the time and effort required to create this book.

- Special appreciation goes to Mr. Ola from Africa, whose insightful feedback and expertise in the tech industry significantly enriched the content of this book. Your contributions were truly invaluable.

- I also want to express my thanks to all my friends, colleagues, and mentors who provided valuable insights, feedback, and encouragement at various stages of this project.

- To the readers who invest their time in exploring the ideas and strategies within these pages, your interest and trust are greatly appreciated.

- Last but not least, I want to acknowledge the entire team at SEO FREQUENCY for their hard work and dedication in bringing this book to fruition.

To everyone who played a role, no matter how big or small, in making this book a reality, your support has been essential in shaping the ideas presented in these pages.

Thank you,

Akram Abbasi
CEO,
SEO FREQUENCY

[January, 2026]

ABOUT THE AUTHOR

It is with great enthusiasm that we introduce the author of the groundbreaking book, "SEO MASTERY: CUTTING EDGE STRATEGIES FOR DOMINATING SEARCH ENGINES." With a remarkable journey spanning the realms of Software Development, Design, and Cyber Academia, this author has distilled their profound knowledge and experiences into a book that promises both enlightenment and motivation.

Throughout their illustrious career, they have consistently demonstrated an unwavering commitment to the forefront of technological evolution. Holding pivotal roles such as Software System Analyst, Full Stack Engineer, Team Lead IT, and Senior Software Engineer, their professional journey has traversed renowned organizations across the globe, from Dubai to Washington, D.C.

In these roles, their mission has been to drive innovation, connecting intricate IT systems with ever-evolving business needs. They have played pivotal roles in pioneering projects, ranging from multi-seller e-commerce systems to state-of-the-art call center solutions and groundbreaking marketplace platforms for mobile and broadband services.

Notably, this author has extended their expertise to education, serving as a Visiting Lecturer at the Federal Urdu University of Arts, Science & Technology. Here, they have imparted their wisdom in courses spanning Object-Oriented Software Engineering to Search Engine Optimization.

Their thirst for knowledge and dedication to excellence is underscored by certifications in Mobile Application Development (Android) and Amazon Web Services Developer - Associate, affirming their commitment to perpetual growth.

Beyond their technical acumen, this author has ventured into the dynamic realm of digital marketing, with a particular focus on the era of AI. Their book, "SEO MASTERY: CUTTING EDGE STRATEGIES FOR DOMINATING SEARCH ENGINES," stands as a testament to their passion for knowledge-sharing and guiding readers through the ever-evolving landscape of digital marketing.

As you delve into the pages of their book, prepare for a transformative journey. Through their words, you'll uncover invaluable insights, strategies, and a renewed perspective on digital marketing in the era of artificial intelligence. This author's unswerving commitment to technology's cutting edge will undoubtedly ignite your own drive to conquer the digital marketing landscape.

Prepare to unveil the secrets of digital success with "SEO MASTERY: CUTTING EDGE STRATEGIES FOR DOMINATING SEARCH ENGINES," authored by an individual whose fervor for technology and innovation knows no bounds.

INTRODUCTION

Have you ever dreamt of soaring above your competition, conquering search engines, and basking in the radiant glow of top rankings? Picture yourself as the ruler of the digital realm, commanding an army of organic traffic like never before. It's a beautiful vision, isn't it? Well, my dear reader, allow me to introduce you to the world of SEO Mastery, where dreams transform into reality, and online success becomes the stuff of legends.

In this humble tome of knowledge and expertise, I invite you to embark on a journey that will forever change the trajectory of your digital presence. Together, we will uncover the secrets, strategies, and techniques that will elevate your website to unprecedented heights. Whether you're a seasoned SEO professional, a curious novice, or someone with an insatiable thirst for knowledge, this book is your sacred map to conquering the search engine battlefield.

But first, let's pause for a moment and marvel at the astonishing power of search engine optimization, or SEO for short. In this ever-evolving digital landscape, where billions of websites compete for attention, SEO stands as the mighty cornerstone of successful online marketing. Just imagine the vast ocean of possibilities that await you once you grasp the intricacies of SEO and ride its waves to uncharted territories.

Now, you may be wondering, what makes this book so different? Why should you entrust your SEO aspirations to the delicate fingers of my words? Allow me to put your mind at ease, my dear reader. Within the pages of "SEO Mastery: Cutting-Edge Strategies for Dominating Search Engines," your fate will be forever altered. The knowledge contained within these chapters is both cutting-edge and revolutionary, designed to arm you with the most effective strategies that will propel your online presence to new heights.

From the moment you crack open this book, you will be transported to the forefront of SEO innovation. We will dive headfirst into the world of cutting-edge techniques that are reshaping the very foundation of the industry. Together, we will harness the ethereal power of artificial intelligence, dance within the realms of user intent optimization, and embrace the mobile-first indexing revolution. Are you ready to leave your competitors in the dust? Buckle up, my friend, for this journey is about to get exhilarating.

But hold on, dear reader, for our adventure has only just begun. Picture yourself as a masterful wordsmith, weaving your way through the labyrinth of content creation. In this book, we will unlock the art of crafting content that not only captivates your audience but also dances gracefully with search engine algorithms. It's a delicate balance, like a waltz in the moonlight, where every step must be strategically chosen to delight both humans and machines. Together, we will unravel the secrets of keyword-rich content and discover how to create an irresistible symphony that resonates with the hearts and minds of readers and search engines alike.

Ah, but what about the technical aspects of SEO, you ask? Fear not, for our journey will take us deep into the mysterious realm of technical wizardry. We will illuminate the path to website optimization, ensuring that your digital abode is a sanctuary for both users and search engines alike. Say goodbye to sluggish load times and bid farewell to labyrinthine site structures. With our guidance, you will emerge as a web architect, empowered to design a user-friendly and search engine-friendly oasis that beckons visitors from every corner of the digital universe.

But wait, there's more! Our journey through the corridors of SEO Mastery will also unveil the enchanting power of local SEO domination. Whether you seek to drive foot traffic to your brick-and-mortar sanctuary or forge connections with local audiences online, this book holds the keys to unlocking the immense potential of local SEO. Discover the secrets to putting your business on the map, both metaphorically and geographically, and watch as your digital kingdom flourishes like never before.

And my dear reader, let us not forget the ever-shifting landscapes of search engine algorithms. With each passing day, a new update emerges, eager to challenge the very foundations of our SEO prowess. But fear not, for within these pages, we will deconstruct these algorithm updates, revealing the hidden treasures they hold and teaching you how to adapt, evolve, and thrive in this ever-changing landscape. Stay informed, my fellow adventurer, for knowledge is the shield that will protect you from obscurity.

But what good is all this knowledge if we cannot measure our progress? Fear not, for we shall embark upon a data-driven journey towards SEO excellence. Arm yourself with the tools and techniques to track your progress, measure your return on investment, and make informed decisions that lead to continuous improvement. Leave no stone unturned, my dear reader, for every piece of data holds the secret to unlocking your true potential.

So, my fellow digital dreamers, brace yourselves for a transformative journey through the pages of "SEO Mastery: Cutting-Edge Strategies for Dominating Search Engines." Written with love, wisdom, and a touch of whimsy, this book is your golden ticket to mastering the intricate dance between search engines and human hearts. Whether you're a business owner seeking to soar above your competitors, a marketing professional eager to sharpen your SEO skills, or an aspiring SEO guru ready to embrace your destiny, this book is your key to unlocking the secrets of the digital realm.

Are you ready to not just play the SEO game, but master it? Are you prepared to unleash the full potential of your digital presence and transform it into a formidable force to be reckoned with? Dive into the pages of "SEO Mastery," my dear reader, and let our adventure begin. Together, we will conquer search engines, rewrite the rules, and forge a new destiny in the boundless expanse of

ANATOMY SEO (SEARCH ENGINE OPTIMIZATION)

1. **Crawling and Indexing**:
2. **On-Page SEO**:
3. **Off-Page SEO**:
4. **Technical SEO**:
5. **Keyword Research**:
6. **User Experience (UX)**:
7. **Content Optimization**:
8. **Local SEO**:
9. **Analytics and Monitoring**:
10. **Algorithm Updates**:

THE ROI OF SEO

As a digital marketing specialist with years of experience in search engine optimization, I am often asked about the return on investment (ROI) of SEO. People want to know if investing time and resources into optimizing their websites for search engines is worth it. The short answer is yes, but with a caveat - it's not an overnight success. SEO is a long-term game, but the rewards it brings can be significant.

Let's dive deeper into the benefits of investing in SEO and how it can contribute to your business's growth. First and foremost, SEO can drive revenue. By optimizing your website for search engines, you make it easier for potential customers to find you when they are actively searching for products or services that you offer. In fact, research shows that organic search traffic has a higher conversion rate compared to other channels, such as social

THE EVOLUTION OF SEO

Let's travel back in time to the early days when SEO was still a novel concept. In the late 1990s, search engines were rudimentary compared to the sophisticated algorithms we see today. Google had just emerged on the scene, and website owners were starting to recognize the importance of having their pages rank on search engine results pages (SERPs) to drive organic traffic. This was the humble beginning of what we now know as search engine optimization.

In its early stages, SEO was relatively straightforward. The focus was primarily on keyword optimization, meta tags, and links. It was all about ensuring that the right keywords were strategically placed throughout a website's content and meta tags to improve visibility on search engines. Additionally, website owners began to optimize their link structures to gain authority and relevance. These techniques proved to be highly effective during this era, but they were just the tip of the iceberg.

The late 90s and early 2000s saw a surge in the number of businesses recognizing the potential of the internet and the need for online visibility. This prompted search engines to continuously refine their algorithms to deliver better results. In turn, SEO professionals had to adapt and hone their skills to stay ahead of these evolving algorithms.

One significant milestone in the history of SEO was the introduction of Google's PageRank algorithm. This revolutionary new system evaluated websites based on the quality and quantity of inbound links. Suddenly, link building became crucial, and SEO professionals were exploring new ways to acquire authoritative and high-quality backlinks. Drawing attention to the importance of content quality, search engines started to evaluate websites based on not only their technical optimization but also the relevance and value it provided to users.

The mid-2000s marked a turning point in the evolution of SEO. The introduction of personalized search results, the rise of social media, and the advent of mobile devices added new dimensions to the SEO landscape. Search engines started using data obtained from the behavior of individual users to deliver more personalized and location-based search results. This shift had a profound impact on the way SEO professionals approached their strategies.

Social media platforms, too, began playing a critical role in influencing search engine rankings. Shares, likes, and comments on platforms like Facebook and Twitter started to impact a website's visibility on SERPs. SEO professionals realized that harnessing the power of social media could amplify their efforts and reach a broader audience. It became apparent that an effective SEO strategy had to extend beyond traditional on-page optimization and delve into the intricacies of social media marketing.

The smartphone revolution further disrupted the SEO landscape. As more people started using mobile devices to search and browse the internet, search engines had to adapt to this new trend. Mobile-friendliness became a ranking factor, urging website owners to ensure their sites were optimized for mobile devices. Google introduced the Mobile-Friendly Update, often referred to as Mobilegeddon, which penalized websites that failed to provide a smooth mobile experience.

Fast forward to the present day, and we find

ourselves navigating the ever-changing world of SEO. Search engines like Google have become smarter, employing artificial intelligence and machine learning to better understand user intent and deliver personalized results. SEO professionals have had to continually evolve their strategies to keep up with this ever-evolving landscape.

One notable recent development is the shift towards user experience (UX) optimization. Search engines now prioritize websites that offer seamless navigation, fast load times, and high-quality content. Factors such as bounce rate, time spent on site, and click-through rate have become critical indicators of a website's overall performance and user satisfaction. Consequently, SEO professionals now invest significant effort in improving user experience, making their strategies more holistic and user-centric.

The influence of voice search technology is yet another game-changer. With the advent of virtual assistants like Siri, Alexa, and Google Assistant, users are increasingly using voice commands to search for information. This shift towards voice search has forced SEO professionals to optimize their content to cater to these voice queries, which often differ from traditional typed searches. Long-tail keywords and natural language processing have become more important in capturing these voice-based searches.

As we delve deeper into the digital age, it's essential to stay on top of the latest developments in SEO. The SEO landscape will continue to evolve, and staying ahead of the curve is crucial for anyone looking to dominate search engine rankings. It's impossible to predict with certainty what the future holds, but one thing is for sure: SEO will continue to play a vital role in the ever-expanding realm of digital marketing.

The Evolution of SEO (Search Engine Optimization) has gone through several phases over the years, each with its own level of importance and strategies. Here's an overview of these phases along with brief examples:

1. **The Early Days (1990s - 2000s):**
2. **The Age of Link Building (2000s - Early 2010s):**
3. **The Era of Content Quality (2010s - Early 2020s):**
4. **Mobile Optimization (2015 - 2020s):**
5. **The Age of User Experience (2020s - Present):**
6. **Voice Search and AI (2020s - Present):**
7. **Local SEO and E-A-T (Expertise, Authoritativeness, Trustworthiness) (Ongoing):**
8. **Video and Visual Search (Ongoing):**

SEO is a dynamic field that continues to evolve, driven by changes in search engine algorithms and user behavior. Staying up-to-date with these developments and adapting strategies accordingly is key to SEO success in the ever-changing digital landscape.

ANATOMY OF SEARCH ENGINES

1: The Building Blocks of Search

Section 1: A Brief History of Search

Section 2: The Indexing Process

Section 3: Understanding Search Algorithms

2: Optimizing for Search Engines

Section 1: On-Page Optimization

Section 2: Off-Page Optimization

Section 3: Mobile Optimization

3: Staying Ahead of the Curve

Section 1: Monitoring and Analyzing Performance

Section 2: Embracing Emerging Technologies

Section 3: The Future of Search

Conclusion

This expanded outline should provide a more comprehensive structure for your book, incorporating examples and insights from the ever-evolving world of SEO.

media or paid advertising.

When your website appears at the top of search engine results pages (SERPs), it lends credibility to your business. Consumers trust search engines to deliver relevant and trustworthy results, so being ranked highly in SERPs can help build trust in your brand. This increased trust can, in turn, lead to higher conversion rates and more sales.

But SEO isn't just about driving immediate revenue. It can also increase brand visibility and awareness in the long run. When your website consistently appears in search results for relevant keywords, it helps build brand recognition and familiarity. Even if users don't click on your website right away, they become aware of your brand's presence and may be more likely to consider it in the future.

The benefits of SEO extend beyond just revenue generation and brand visibility. It can also contribute to long-term business growth. When you have a solid SEO strategy in place, you are continuously optimizing your website for search engines, making it easier for potential customers to find you. This consistent focus on SEO can lead to sustainable growth over time. As your website climbs higher in the search rankings, you will attract more organic traffic, which can result in increased sales and revenue.

Moreover, SEO is a cost-effective marketing strategy compared to other digital marketing channels. While paid advertising can bring immediate results, it requires ongoing investment to maintain visibility. SEO, on the other hand, can continue to deliver results even after the initial optimization work is done. Though it may require periodic updates and adjustments, the long-term benefits of SEO can outweigh the cost.

To better understand the ROI of SEO, let's consider a hypothetical scenario. Imagine you have a small online retail business selling handmade jewelry. Without any SEO efforts, your website is buried on the 10th page of search results, making it nearly impossible for potential customers to find you. However, by implementing an SEO strategy that includes keyword research, on-page optimization, and link building, you manage to improve your website's ranking and appear on the first page of search results for relevant keywords.

As a result of this improved visibility, your website sees a significant increase in organic traffic. More people are discovering your business, browsing your products, and making purchases. This surge in sales directly impacts your revenue and helps your business grow. Additionally, as more people become aware of your brand through search, your overall brand awareness and recognition increase, potentially leading to repeat business and word-of-mouth referrals.

The benefits of SEO are not limited to specific industries or businesses. Whether you are a small local business or a multinational corporation, investing in SEO can provide substantial returns. The key is to develop a well-rounded SEO strategy that aligns with your business goals, incorporates the latest SEO trends, and adapts to the ever-evolving search landscape.

In conclusion, investing in SEO can yield a significant return on investment in terms of revenue, brand visibility, and long-term business growth. By optimizing your website for search engines, you can make it easier for potential customers to find you, build trust in your brand, and drive sustainable organic traffic. While SEO is a long-term game, the benefits it brings make it a worthwhile investment for any business looking to dominate search engines and stay ahead of the competition.

Remember, SEO is not a one-time effort but an ongoing process. It requires constant monitoring, analysis, and adaptation to stay relevant in the ever-changing world of search engines. By staying up to date with the latest SEO strategies and best practices, you can maximize your ROI and unlock the full potential of SEO for your business. So, start investing in SEO today and watch your business thrive in the digital landscape.

The Return on Investment (ROI) of SEO, often called "The ROI of SEO," is a crucial metric for businesses that invest in search engine optimization. SEO is essential because it helps improve a website's visibility on search engines like Google, leading to more organic traffic, better user experiences, and ultimately, higher revenue. Let's delve into the importance of SEO with some brief examples:

In conclusion, the ROI of SEO lies in its ability to drive organic traffic, enhance user experiences, and provide a sustainable, cost-effective marketing strategy. It empowers businesses to compete effectively in the digital landscape and expand their reach, ultimately leading to increased revenue and growth.

2

Cutting-Edge SEO Techniques

AI-POWERED SEO

Introduction:

As the world of technology continues to evolve, so does the field of search engine optimization (SEO). Gone are the days of relying solely on keyword optimization and backlink strategies to improve website rankings. The emergence of artificial intelligence (AI) and machine learning algorithms has revolutionized the way we approach SEO. In this chapter, we will delve into the power of AI and explore how it can optimize websites through the analysis of user behavior.

Section 1: Understanding Artificial Intelligence in SEO

1.1 The Rise of AI:

Artificial intelligence has rapidly gained popularity in recent years, transforming various industries and bringing about unparalleled advancements. In the realm of SEO, AI has become a game-changer. With its ability to process enormous amounts of data and make intelligent predictions, AI has become an indispensable tool for marketers and website owners.

1.2 Machine Learning Algorithms:

At the heart of AI-powered SEO lies machine learning algorithms. These algorithms can analyze vast sets of data, including user behavior, to understand patterns and trends that influence search engine rankings. By leveraging machine learning, marketers can gain valuable insights into their target audience and optimize their websites accordingly.

Section 2: Harnessing AI for SEO Success

2.1 Analyzing User Behavior:

Understanding how users interact with a website is crucial for SEO success. AI-powered tools can track user engagement metrics, such as click-through rates, bounce rates, and time spent on page, enabling marketers to identify areas for improvement. By analyzing user behavior, AI can help optimize website design, navigation, and content placement to provide a seamless user experience.

2.2 Predicting Search Intent:

Accurately predicting search intent is paramount in creating relevant and valuable content. AI-powered SEO tools can analyze search queries and understand the underlying intent behind them. By understanding user intent, marketers can create content that meets their needs, ultimately improving search engine rankings.

2.3 Content Creation and Optimization:

AI can also play a significant role in content creation and optimization. Natural language processing algorithms can analyze existing content and identify opportunities for improvement, such as optimizing meta tags, headers, and keyword usage. Additionally, AI-powered tools can generate content ideas based on trending topics and user preferences, assisting marketers in creating engaging and SEO-friendly content.

Section 3: AI-Powered SEO Implementation

3.1 Structured Data Markup:

Structured data markup provides search engines with metadata about a website's content, making it easier for them to understand and index the site. AI-powered SEO tools can analyze the structure of a website and recommend appropriate markup, enhancing visibility and search engine rankings.

3.2 Voice Search Optimization:

With the rise of voice assistants and smart

devices, optimizing for voice search has become essential. AI-powered SEO tools can analyze voice search patterns and provide insights on how to optimize content for voice queries. By adapting to the changing search landscape, website owners can ensure they remain competitive in the era of AI and voice search.

Section 4: Future Possibilities and Challenges

4.1 AI-Driven Personalization:

AI has the potential to revolutionize personalized search experiences. With AI algorithms tracking user preferences, websites can deliver customized content based on individual interests, search history, and behavior patterns. By leveraging AI-driven personalization, marketers can provide tailored recommendations and enhance user engagement.

4.2 Ethical and Privacy Concerns:

As AI continues to advance, ethical and privacy concerns come to the forefront. It is crucial for website owners and marketers to balance the benefits of AI-powered SEO with respect for user privacy. Transparency and responsible data handling must be maintained to build trust with users and ensure the ethical use of AI technologies.

Conclusion:

In conclusion, AI-powered SEO is changing the

game for marketers and website owners. By leveraging the power of artificial intelligence and machine learning algorithms, marketers can gain valuable insights into user behavior and optimize their websites for improved search engine rankings. From analyzing user behavior to predicting search intent and optimizing content, AI is revolutionizing the field of SEO. However, it is essential to approach AI-powered SEO with ethical considerations and privacy concerns in mind. As technology continues to evolve, embracing AI can pave the way for SEO mastery and successful online visibility in the ever-changing digital landscape.

AI-powered SEO, which combines the capabilities of artificial intelligence with search engine optimization, has become increasingly crucial in the digital marketing landscape. AI can help streamline processes, gather data, and make data-driven decisions to improve a website's visibility in search engine results pages. Here's a breakdown of AI-powered SEO and its importance, along with brief examples:

1. Content Optimization:

2. Predictive Analytics:

3. Natural Language Processing (NLP):

4. Rank Tracking and Monitoring:

5. Content Generation:

6. Personalization:

7. Technical SEO:

8. Voice Search Optimization:

AI-powered SEO is a dynamic field, and it continues to evolve as AI technologies become more sophisticated. By harnessing the power of AI in SEO, businesses can improve their online visibility, attract more organic traffic, and deliver a better user experience.

USER INTENT OPTIMIZATION

As a digital marketer, I have always emphasized the importance of understanding user intent when it comes to SEO. Gone are the days when simply stuffing keywords into your content would guarantee top rankings on search engine results pages (SERPs). Today, search engines have become smarter, and they prioritize user experience above all else. In this chapter, I will delve deep into the concept of user intent optimization and explain how aligning your content with the needs and expectations of your target audience can lead to higher rankings and better conversions.

Section 1: Defining User Intent

User intent refers to the underlying purpose or goal behind a user's search query. Understanding user intent helps us uncover the true meaning behind a search and enables us to deliver relevant content that satisfies the user's needs. There are generally four types of user intent:

1. Informational Intent: Users are seeking information or answers to their questions. They may search for product reviews, how-to guides, or general knowledge on a particular topic.

2. Navigational Intent: Users have a specific website or brand in mind and are searching for a particular website or webpage. They may include brand names or domain names in their search query.

3. Transactional Intent: Users are ready to make a purchase or engage in a specific transaction. They may search for product comparisons, discounts, or where to buy a particular product.

4. Commercial Investigation Intent: Users are in the research phase of the buying process and are comparing different products or services. They may search for product reviews, pricing information, or feature comparisons.

Section 2: Aligning Your Content with User Intent

Now that we understand the different types of user intent, it's important to align our content with the specific intent of our target audience. To do this effectively, we need to:

1. Analyze search queries: By analyzing the search queries that bring users to our website, we can gain valuable insights into their intent. Tools like Google Analytics and Google Search Console can provide us with the necessary data to understand what our audience is looking for.

2. Optimize content for specific intent: Once we have identified the user intent behind certain search queries, we can then optimize our content to cater to that intent. For informational intent, we can create in-depth guides or articles that provide valuable information to users. For transactional intent, we can optimize our product pages and include clear calls-to-action to encourage conversions.

3. Use keywords strategically: Keywords are an essential component of SEO, and using them strategically can help align our content with user intent. Long-tail keywords that include specific intent-related phrases can help attract the right audience to our website.

Section 3: Creating Conversion-Focused Content

Optimizing for user intent goes beyond just

ranking well on SERPs. It is equally important to create content that not only ranks well but also converts. Here are some strategies to create conversion-focused content:

1. Understand your target audience: To create content that converts, we need to have a deep understanding of our target audience. What are their pain points? What are their needs and desires? By understanding our audience, we can create content that addresses their specific needs.

2. Use persuasive copywriting techniques: Copywriting plays a crucial role in converting visitors into customers. By using persuasive language, highlighting benefits, and incorporating social proof, we can compel users to take action.

3. Include clear calls-to-action (CTAs): A clear and compelling CTA can make all the difference in converting a visitor. Make sure your CTAs stand out, are strategically placed, and clearly communicate the intended action.

4. Optimize for mobile: With the rise of mobile usage, it is crucial to optimize your content for mobile devices. A mobile-friendly website and content that is easy to read and navigate on smaller screens can significantly improve conversions.

Conclusion:

In today's competitive digital landscape, understanding user intent is crucial for SEO success. By aligning our content with the needs and expectations of our target audience, we can not only rank well on SERPs but also increase conversions. Remember, it's not just about getting traffic to your website; it's about attracting the right audience and providing them with a valuable and conversion-focused experience.

User Intent Optimization is a crucial aspect of SEO (Search Engine Optimization) as it focuses on understanding and catering to the specific needs and intentions of users when they perform online searches. By aligning your content with user intent, you can improve your website's visibility in search results and enhance the overall user experience. Here's a breakdown of the concept along with brief examples:

1. **Informational Intent**:
2. **Navigational Intent**:
3. **Transactional Intent**:
4. **Commercial Investigation Intent**:
5. **Local Intent**:
6. **Educational Intent**:

7. Long-Tail Keywords and Voice Search:

Remember that understanding and optimizing for user intent is an ongoing process. Regularly analyze your website's performance and user behavior to refine your SEO strategy and ensure that your content aligns with the evolving needs and intentions of your target audience.

MOBILE-FIRST
INDEXING

A s a savvy marketer or website owner, it is crucial to recognize and embrace the mobile revolution. The growing number of mobile users means that your website must be optimized for mobile-first indexing. In other words, search engines are prioritizing the mobile version of websites over the desktop version when crawling and ranking search results. This shift signifies a fundamental change in the way search engines view the importance of mobile usability and user experience.

To stay ahead of the competition and ensure maximum visibility in search engine rankings, it is imperative to adopt mobile-first indexing strategies that align with the ever-evolving demands of mobile users. In this chapter, we will delve deep into various techniques to optimize your website for mobile-first indexing, enhance mobile user experience, improve site speed, and ultimately boost search engine rankings on mobile devices.

STEP 1:

RESPONSIVE WEB DESIGN

T he first step in embracing the mobile revolution is to ensure that your website has a responsive design. Responsive web design is a method of designing and developing websites that adapt to the size and orientation of the user's device, providing an optimal user experience on both mobile and desktop devices. This approach eliminates the need for separate mobile and desktop versions of your website, streamlining the maintenance process and improving consistency across all platforms.

By incorporating responsive design principles into your website, you can ensure that it not only looks visually appealing on mobile devices but also functions seamlessly. This means that all the elements of your website, including images, text, and navigation menus, should adapt and adjust automatically to fit the screen size of the user's device. A responsive website will not only enhance mobile user experience but also send positive signals to search engines that your website is mobile-friendly.

STEP 2:

OPTIMIZE FOR MOBILE USER EXPERIENCE

Mobile users value speed, simplicity, and ease of navigation. To create a delightful mobile user experience, you need to optimize your website accordingly. Start by prioritizing the most critical content and features of your website, ensuring that they are easily accessible on mobile devices.

Consider implementing mobile-friendly navigation menus that are intuitive and simple to use, such as a hamburger menu or a fixed navigation bar at the top of the screen. These navigation options ensure that users can easily navigate through your website, find the information they need, and take desired actions without frustration.

Additionally, make sure that your website loads quickly on mobile devices. Slow-loading websites are a major turn-off for mobile users who demand instant gratification. Optimize your images, minify your HTML, CSS, and JavaScript files, and leverage caching techniques to reduce page load times. Remember, the faster your website loads, the higher the chances of retaining your mobile visitors and boosting your search engine rankings.

STEP 3:

MOBILE-
FRIENDLY
CONTENT

When it comes to mobile-first indexing, content is still king. However, mobile users consume content differently than desktop users. To effectively engage and captivate mobile users, you need to adapt your content strategy accordingly.

Firstly, ensure that your content is formatted

for mobile devices. Use shorter paragraphs, bullet points, and subheadings to break up the text and make it easier to read on smaller screens. Avoid using large blocks of text, as they can be overwhelming and discourage mobile users from engaging with your content.

Secondly, optimize your images for mobile devices by using appropriate file formats and reducing their size without compromising quality. Large and cumbersome images can slow down your website and hinder mobile user experience. By compressing images and using modern file formats such as WebP, you can significantly improve load times and ensure a smooth browsing experience for your mobile visitors.

Lastly, consider incorporating video content into your mobile strategy. Video consumption on mobile devices has skyrocketed in recent years, and users often prefer watching videos rather than reading lengthy articles. Take advantage of this trend by creating engaging and relevant video content that complements your written content.

STEP 4: ACCELERATED MOBILE PAGES (AMP)

T o take your mobile optimization efforts to the next level, consider implementing Accelerated Mobile Pages (AMP) on your website. AMP is an open-source initiative led by Google and other prominent tech companies, aimed at creating lightning-fast web pages that load almost instantly on mobile devices.

Implementing AMP involves creating streamlined versions of your web pages that strip away unnecessary elements and prioritize speed. By using various optimization techniques, such as prerendering, lazy loading, and efficient caching, AMP pages can provide a seamless and blazing-fast browsing experience for mobile users.

Furthermore, AMP pages are favored by search engines, as they are designed to meet strict performance criteria. Implementing AMP on your website can boost your search engine rankings and attract more organic traffic from mobile users who value speed and efficiency.

STEP 5:

STRUCTURED DATA FOR MOBILE SEARCH RESULTS

Structured data, also known as schema markup, is a powerful tool that allows you to provide search engines with additional context and information about your website's content. By implementing structured data, you can enhance the visibility and appearance of your website in search engine results pages (SERPs).

When it comes to mobile-first indexing, structured data can be a game-changer. By marking up your content with relevant structured data, you can improve its chances of being featured in mobile search results. Rich snippets, knowledge panels, and other visually appealing search features can significantly enhance the visibility and click-through rates of your website on mobile devices.

Take advantage of schema.org and other structured data markup languages to annotate your content with relevant metadata. By providing search engines with structured data, you are effectively helping them understand the context and relevance of your content, resulting in better rankings and increased traffic from mobile users.

STEP 6:

MOBILE
SITE SPEED
OPTIMIZATION

I n the mobile-first era, website speed is more critical than ever before. Mobile users have little patience for slow-loading websites, and search engines recognize this by incorporating site speed as a ranking factor. Improving your website's mobile site speed should be a top priority if you want to dominate search engine rankings on mobile devices.

Start by conducting a mobile site speed audit to identify areas for improvement. Tools such as Google's PageSpeed Insights and GTmetrix provide valuable insights into your website's performance on mobile devices and suggest optimizations.

Optimizing images, minifying CSS and JavaScript files, leveraging browser caching, and reducing the number of HTTP requests are just a few techniques that can drastically improve your website's mobile site speed. As a rule of thumb, aim for a load time of under three seconds, as this is the threshold at which mobile users typically begin to abandon a website.

STEP 7: MONITOR AND ITERATE

I n the ever-evolving landscape of mobile-first indexing, staying ahead of the curve requires constant monitoring and iteration. Monitor your website's performance on mobile devices by analyzing metrics such as bounce rate, time on page, and conversions specific to mobile users.

Leverage tools such as Google Analytics and Google Search Console to gain valuable insights into user behavior on your website across different devices. Use these insights to identify areas for improvement and iterate on your mobile optimization strategies accordingly.

Additionally, stay up-to-date with the latest mobile-first indexing trends and algorithm updates by following reputable SEO blogs and industry publications. Search engine algorithms are constantly evolving, and staying informed will enable you to adapt your mobile optimization strategies to align with the latest best practices.

Embrace the Mobile Revolution

The rise of mobile usage has forever changed the way we interact with the online world. As search engines continue to prioritize the mobile version of websites, it is crucial to embrace the mobile revolution and optimize your website for mobile-first indexing. By following the steps outlined in this chapter, you can improve mobile user experience, increase site speed, and ultimately dominate search engine rankings on mobile devices. Remember, the future is mobile, and those who embrace it will reap the rewards of a digital world that is always at their fingertips.

Mobile-First Indexing is a critical aspect of modern SEO, emphasizing the importance of mobile-friendly websites in search engine rankings. Here's a breakdown of its significance with brief examples:

In summary, Mobile-First Indexing underscores the need for websites to prioritize mobile users, not only for better search engine rankings but also to deliver an improved user experience. Optimizing for mobile responsiveness, site speed, and user engagement can have a significant impact on your SEO performance in today's mobile-centric digital landscape.

3

Crafting Compelling Content

KEYWORD RESEARCH AND OPTIMIZATION

As an avid marketer and SEO enthusiast, I've come to understand that mastering the art of keyword research and optimization is crucial to achieving success in the digital landscape. In this chapter, I will guide you through a step-by-step process that will empower you to identify high-value keywords, seamlessly integrate them into your content, and ultimately increase your organic traffic. So, let's dive in and explore the world of keyword research and optimization.

STEP 1:

UNDERSTANDIN G THE IMPORTANCE OF KEYWORD RESEARCH

Before we delve into the intricacies of keyword research and optimization, it's essential to grasp the fundamental role that keywords play in the search engine ecosystem. Keywords act as a bridge between users and search engines, enabling them to match queries with relevant content. By strategically incorporating high-value keywords into your content, you can increase your chances of ranking well in search engine results pages (SERPs) and attract highly targeted organic traffic.

STEP 2:

CONDUCTING THOROUGH KEYWORD RESEARCH

Now that we understand the significance of keyword research, let's explore how to identify the most valuable keywords for your content. This step requires a combination of creativity, analysis, and intuition to uncover the keywords that align with your target audience's search intent.

To begin, put yourself in the shoes of your target audience. What words or phrases would they use to find the type of content you are providing? Brainstorm a variety of potential keywords and phrases that reflect your content's topic or theme. Once you have a list, it's time to dive deeper into keyword research tools to validate and expand upon your initial ideas.

Keyword research tools, such as Google Keyword Planner, SEMrush, or Ahrefs, are invaluable resources to help you uncover related keywords, estimate search volumes, assess competition, and identify trends. Utilize these tools to refine and expand your list of potential keywords, focusing on those that have high search volumes and low competition.

STEP 3:

ANALYZING COMPETITORS AND IDENTIFYING GAPS

In the ever-evolving world of SEO, keeping an eye on your competitors is crucial. By analyzing their keyword strategies, you gain valuable insights that can help you improve your own keyword optimization.

Examine the SERPs for your target keywords and

pay attention to the types of content that are ranking well. Identify patterns and commonalities in their keyword usage, content structure, and overall approach. Next, analyze their backlink profiles to gain a deeper understanding of how they are acquiring high-quality links.

By studying your competitors, you can identify potential gaps in their strategies that you can leverage to gain a competitive advantage. Look for keywords that your competitors are poorly targeting or not targeting at all. These gaps present a unique opportunity to create content that fills the void and attracts highly relevant organic traffic.

STEP 4:

INTEGRATING KEYWORDS SEAMLESSLY INTO YOUR CONTENT

Now that you have a comprehensive list of high-value keywords, it's time to integrate them seamlessly into your content. Keyword optimization involves striking the delicate balance between catering to search engines' algorithms and providing valuable, engaging content for your audience.

Start by selecting a primary keyword for each piece of content. This keyword should encapsulate the main topic and be highly relevant to your target audience. Ensure that your chosen keyword is present in your title, Meta tags, headers, and throughout the body of your content. However, be cautious not to overuse keywords, as this can be perceived as spammy by search engines and negatively impact your rankings.

In addition to your primary keyword, incorporate related keywords and synonyms into your content. This helps search engines understand the context and depth of your content, boosting your chances of ranking well for a broader range of search queries.

Remember, the goal is not just to rank well; it's to provide valuable and informative content that meets the expectations of your audience. So, while keywords are important, prioritize the user experience above all else.

STEP 5:

MONITORING AND ITERATING YOUR KEYWORD STRATEGY

In the world of SEO, continuous improvement is crucial. Once you've implemented your keyword optimization strategy, it's crucial to monitor its performance and make necessary adjustments along the way.

Leverage analytics tools to track the organic traffic and engagement metrics of your optimized content. Identify any fluctuations in rankings, click-through rates (CTRs), or bounce rates, and use this data to refine and enhance your keyword strategy. Experiment with different variations of keywords, content formats, and approaches to ensure you are continuously optimizing your content for maximum visibility and impact.

Conclusion

Mastering the art of keyword research and optimization is not an exact science, but rather an ongoing journey of discovery and improvement. By following the step-by-step guide outlined in this chapter, you'll be equipped with the knowledge and tools necessary to elevate your content's visibility in search engine results and drive targeted organic traffic to your website. Remember, SEO is a dynamic field, so never stop exploring, experimenting, and fine-tuning your keyword strategy to stay ahead of the curve and dominate the search engine landscape.

Keyword research and optimization are essential components of SEO (Search Engine Optimization) that help improve your website's visibility in search engine results pages. Here's a guide to keyword research and optimization, along with brief examples:

Keyword Research:

1. **Understand Your Audience:**

- Identify your target audience and their search intent. What are they looking for? What problems do they want to solve? Example: If you run a fitness blog, your audience might be interested in weight loss tips and workout routines.

2. **Brainstorm Seed Keywords:**

   - Create a list of general, high-level keywords relevant to your content or business. Example: "Fitness," "Weight Loss," "Healthy Eating."

3. **Use Keyword Research Tools:**

   - Utilize tools like Google Keyword Planner, SEMrush, or Ahrefs to discover related keywords and their search volumes. Example: Discover that "low-carb diet" has a high search volume.

4. **Analyze Keyword Competition:**

   - Assess the competitiveness of keywords by examining the search results and the websites ranking for them. Example: Highly competitive keywords might be dominated by authoritative websites.

5. **Long-Tail Keywords:**

   - Incorporate long-tail keywords (more specific, longer phrases) that cater to niche queries. Example: "Low-carb diet meal plan for beginners" is a long-tail keyword.

Keyword Optimization:

1. **On-Page Optimization:**
   - Place your target keyword strategically in the following on-page elements: Title tag, Meta description, Headings (H1, H2, H3), URL structure, and within the content itself. Example: If your keyword is "low-carb diet," ensure it appears naturally in these elements.

2. **Content Quality:**
   - Create high-quality, informative, and engaging content that satisfies the user's search intent. Example: Provide in-depth information about low-carb diets, their benefits, and meal plans.

3. **Avoid Keyword Stuffing:**
   - Don't overuse keywords. Ensure your content reads naturally and doesn't sound spammy. Example: Instead of saying, "Looking for a low-carb diet? Our low-carb diet plan is the best low-carb diet for you," say, "Our low-carb diet plan is designed to help you achieve your fitness goals."

4. **Mobile Optimization:**
   - Optimize your website for mobile devices, as Google considers mobile-friendliness when ranking sites. Example: Ensure responsive design and fast loading times on mobile

devices.

5. **Local SEO:**

   - If applicable, include location-based keywords for local SEO. Example: "Best fitness trainer in New York" for a local fitness trainer's website.

6. **Regular Updates:**

   - Keep your content up to date and relevant to maintain search engine rankings. Example: Update your fitness blog with the latest diet trends and exercise routines.

7. **User Experience:**

   - Ensure a user-friendly website with clear navigation and fast loading times. Example: A well-structured site encourages users to stay and explore further.

8. **Backlinks:**

   - Build high-quality backlinks from reputable websites to increase your site's authority. Example: Guest post on fitness-related websites with a link back to your content.

Remember that SEO is an ongoing process, and regular monitoring and adjustments are crucial to maintaining and improving your search rankings. Additionally, search engine algorithms evolve, so staying updated with SEO best practices is essential for long-term success.

CREATING ENGAGING BLOG POSTS

STEP 1:

STRUCTURING YOUR POSTS

When it comes to creating engaging blog posts, the structure is key. No matter how brilliant your content is, if it's poorly organized, readers will quickly lose interest. To structure your posts effectively, start with a compelling headline that grabs your audience's attention and entices them to click.

Next, divide your content into clear and concise paragraphs. Each paragraph should focus on a specific idea or topic, making it easier for readers to digest the information. Use subheadings to break up your text and guide readers through the post. This not only makes your content skimmable but also helps with SEO optimization by signaling to search engines what your post is about.

STEP 2:

THE ART OF STORYTELLING

Storytelling is a powerful tool for engaging readers and creating an emotional connection. When crafting your blog posts, aim to tell a compelling story that resonates with your audience. Start by identifying the central message or theme of your post and build your narrative around it.

Introduce your story with a captivating hook that grabs readers' attention and makes them want to know more. Whether it's a personal anecdote, a surprising fact, or an intriguing question, the hook should entice readers to keep reading.

As you progress through your blog post, maintain a consistent narrative that is both relatable and engaging. Use descriptive language and vivid storytelling techniques to paint a picture in your readers' minds, allowing them to visualize the concepts you're presenting.

Whether you're discussing a product, service, or an industry trend, try to incorporate real-life examples and case studies. This adds credibility to your content and helps readers relate to the information you're sharing. It's through relevant and relatable stories that readers can truly connect with your content and find value in what you have to say.

STEP 3:

OPTIMIZE
FOR SEO

While creating engaging blog posts is important, it's equally crucial to optimize your content for search engines. After all, what's the use of a well-crafted post if no one can find it? By strategically incorporating SEO techniques into your blog posts, you can increase their visibility in search engine results and drive more organic traffic to your website.

Start by conducting thorough keyword research to identify the most relevant and high-ranking keywords in your niche. Incorporate these keywords naturally into your content, including in your headings, subheadings, and meta descriptions.

In addition to keywords, pay attention to other on-page SEO elements such as meta titles and meta descriptions. These elements not only provide search engines with valuable information about your content but also entice users to click on your link in search results.

When it comes to optimizing your blog posts, it's import

ant to strike a balance between SEO and user experience. While keywords are important, don't overstuff your content with them. Focus on creating valuable and engaging content that provides real value to your audience.

STEP 4:

ENGAGE WITH YOUR AUDIENCE

E ngaging with your audience is crucial to building a loyal following and driving traffic to your website. Encourage readers to leave comments and engage in discussions by ending your blog posts with a thoughtful question or a call to action.

Responding to comments and actively participating in discussions not only strengthens your relationship with your audience but also signals to search engines that your content is valuable and engaging. This, in turn, can help improve your SEO rankings and drive more traffic to your website.

Furthermore, consider incorporating social sharing buttons into your blog posts. This makes it easier for readers to share your content on various social media platforms, increasing its reach and potential for going viral.

STEP 5:

ANALYZE AND REFINE YOUR APPROACH

Creating engaging blog posts is an ongoing process of learning and refinement. To maximize your blog's impact, regularly analyze your content and its performance. Monitor metrics such as page views, bounce rate, and engagement rate to gain insights into what resonates with your audience and what doesn't.

Based on your analysis, refine your approach and experiment with different techniques. Pay attention to trending topics and innovative storytelling formats that can help you stand out from the crowd.

In conclusion, creating engaging blog posts requires a well-structured approach, the art of storytelling, and strategic SEO optimization. By following these steps and continuously refining your approach, you can captivate your audience, drive traffic to your website, and ultimately dominate search engines. Remember, the key to success lies in providing value, connecting with your readers, and consistently delivering high-quality content.

VIDEO AND VISUAL CONTENT OPTIMIZATION

I n today's digital landscape, visual content has become increasingly important in capturing the attention of online users. With the rise of social media platforms and the popularity of visual-based apps like Instagram and TikTok, it is clear that people are drawn to engaging and visually appealing content. As the saying goes, "a picture is worth a thousand words," and in the realm of SEO, this holds true. In this chapter, we will delve into the world of video and visual content optimization, uncovering the immense power they hold in dominating search engines.

Section 1: Understanding the Power of Video Content

Video content has taken the internet by storm, becoming one of the most engaging and influential forms of digital media. According to recent research, videos account for a significant portion of internet traffic, with a projected 82% by 2022. This staggering statistic highlights the importance of incorporating videos into your SEO strategy. Not only do videos have a higher chance of going viral, but they also have the ability to improve your website's visibility and increase user engagement.

Section 2: Creating Engaging Videos for SEO Success

Creating compelling videos that captivate your audience is essential for achieving SEO success. To begin, it's crucial to define your target audience and understand their preferences and interests. Conducting thorough research will enable you to craft videos that resonate with your intended viewers. Whether it's explainer videos, product demonstrations, or engaging storytelling, tailoring your content to your audience will ensure maximum impact.

Furthermore, it's important to optimize your videos for SEO by utilizing relevant keywords in your video titles, descriptions, and tags. By including keywords that align with your target audience's search queries, you increase the chances of your videos appearing in search engine results pages (SERPs). Additionally, embedding videos directly into your website will enhance user experience and reduce bounce rates, ultimately boosting your search rankings.

Section 3: Mastering Image Alt Tags for Enhanced Visibility

While videos steal the spotlight, images shouldn't be overlooked in your SEO strategy. Search engines not only love visual content but also rely on alt tags to understand the context of your images. Alt tags serve as descriptions for visually impaired users, and they play a vital role in ensuring your images are appropriately indexed and ranked by search engines.

To optimize your images for maximum visibility, start by using descriptive alt tags that accurately convey the content and purpose of the image. Including relevant keywords in the alt tags will further enhance your chances of ranking higher in image search results. Additionally, compressing your images to improve page load times and providing high-quality images that are visually appealing will improve user experience, ultimately contributing to better search rankings.

Section 4: Leveraging Visual Content for Higher Search Rankings

Visual content extends beyond videos and images. Infographics, GIFs, and interactive visual elements have become popular ways to engage users and increase organic traffic. Infographics, in particular, are highly shareable and linkable, making them valuable assets for SEO. By creating visually appealing and informative infographics, you increase the likelihood of earning backlinks from reputable websites, further strengthening your website's authority and search rankings.

Additionally, incorporating visual elements within your written content can break up text, making it more visually appealing and easily digestible for readers. By utilizing headers, bullet points, and eye-catching graphics, you create a visually appealing user experience that encourages readers to stay on your page longer. Higher user engagement and reduced bounce rates are positive signals to search engines, and this can lead to improved search rankings.

In conclusion, video and visual content optimization are crucial components of a successful SEO strategy. By understanding the power of videos, creating engaging content, and optimizing images and visual elements, you increase your chances of dominating search engines. As digital marketing continues to evolve, it's essential to adapt and embrace the visual revolution. After all, a picture is worth a thousand words, and in the world of SEO, it can be worth much more – higher visibility, increased organic traffic, and ultimately, business success.

Stay tuned for the next chapter, where we explore the world of mobile optimization and discuss strategies for dominating search engines in the age of smartphones and mobile devices.

4

TECHNICAL
WIZARDRY

SITE SPEED OPTIMIZATION

In today's fast-paced digital world, every second matters. From impatient internet users to search engine algorithms, everyone demands quick results. As a website owner, it is crucial to recognize the significance of site speed optimization. Not only does it provide a better user experience, but it also plays a vital role in improving search engine rankings.

Imagine visiting a website that takes ages to load. Frustration builds up, and the chances are high that you will abandon that site, never to return again. This is precisely why optimizing your website's loading speed is imperative. Users expect instant access to the information they seek, and failure to deliver on that demand can have severe consequences.

From a search engine perspective, site speed optimization is a key ranking factor. Google, for instance, considers page load time when determining search engine rankings. If your website performs poorly in this regard, it may be penalized and pushed down the search engine results pages (SERPs). On the flip side, a fast-loading website stands a higher chance of reaching the top of the SERPs.

So, how can you ensure that your website's loading speed is in top shape? Let's dive into some step-by-step techniques for effective site speed optimization.

STEP 2:

REDUCING PAGE LOAD TIMES

The first step towards optimizing website speed is to reduce page load times. A slow-loading website can be a major turn-off for visitors, resulting in high bounce rates and lost potential conversions. The key here is to focus on minimizing the elements that contribute to page load times.

One effective technique is to optimize your website's code. Bloated or poorly written code can significantly hinder page load times. By streamlining your code and reducing unnecessary elements, you can create a leaner and faster-loading website.

Another crucial aspect to consider is minimizing the number of HTTP requests. When a user visits your webpage, their browser sends multiple HTTP requests to fetch different website elements, such as images, CSS files, and JavaScript files. The more requests made, the more time it takes for the page to load. By combining, minifying, and compressing these elements, you can significantly reduce the number of HTTP requests and boost page load times.

Additionally, leveraging browser caching can greatly enhance website performance. Browser caching allows returning users to load previously visited pages more quickly by storing certain website resources locally. By setting appropriate expiration dates on these resources, you can ensure that users retrieve updated content while still benefiting from faster load times.

STEP 3:

OPTIMIZE IMAGES FOR FASTER LOADING

I mages play a crucial role in enhancing the visual appeal of a website. However, large image file sizes can significantly slow down page load times. Therefore, optimizing images is a critical step in improving website speed.

The first technique to employ is image compression. There are various tools and plugins available that can compress your images without compromising their quality. By reducing the file size of your images, you can ensure faster load times while maintaining visual appeal.

Another technique is lazy loading. This involves loading images as the user scrolls down the page, rather than loading all of them at once. By implementing lazy loading, you can prioritize the loading of visible content and delay the loading of off-screen images, thus improving overall page load times.

Furthermore, it is important to specify image dimensions in your HTML code. By providing the width and height of each image, you allow the browser to allocate space for the image in advance, preventing layout shifts and reducing page load times.

STEP 4:

LEVERAGE CACHING FOR FASTER WEBSITE PERFORMANCE

C aching is an essential technique that can significantly enhance website performance. By temporarily storing data, caching reduces the need for repeated processing and improves overall speed.

One effective caching technique is leveraging browser caching. As mentioned earlier, setting appropriate expiration dates on website resources allows browsers to store and reuse these resources. By enabling caching headers, you can control how long these resources are stored by the browser, thereby reducing the need for repeated requests.

Server-side caching is another technique that can greatly enhance website speed. By caching the generated HTML output of a page, subsequent visits to that page can be served directly from the cache, eliminating the need for repeated processing. This can be implemented using various caching plugins or server configurations.

CDN (Content Delivery Network) caching is also worth considering. CDN helps distribute your website's content across a network of servers stationed in different geographic locations. This allows users to access your website from a server closest to their location, reducing latency and improving overall site speed.

In Conclusion

Optimizing your website's loading speed is not only crucial for providing a better user experience but also for improving search engine rankings. By following the step-by-step techniques outlined in this chapter, you can significantly enhance your website's performance and ensure faster page load times.

Remember, site speed optimization is an ongoing process. Regularly monitor your website's performance, keep an eye on new optimization techniques, and adapt as necessary. By continuously striving to provide the best possible user experience, you can dominate search engine rankings and stay ahead of the competition in today's digital landscape.

So, dive into the world of site speed optimization and witness the transformative power it can have on your online presence.

Site speed optimization is a crucial factor in SEO, as search engines like Google consider page loading times when ranking websites. A faster website not only improves user experience but also positively impacts your search engine rankings. Here are some key aspects of site speed optimization, along with brief examples:

Example (Apache):

```
<IfModule mod_expires.c>

ExpiresActive On

ExpiresByType image/jpg "access plus 1 year"

ExpiresByType image/jpeg "access plus 1 year"
```

ExpiresByType image/png "access plus 1 year"

</IfModule> **Enable Gzip Compression**: Compress your website's resources using Gzip. This reduces the size of data transferred between the server and the client, speeding up page load times.

Example (Apache):
<IfModule mod_deflate.c>

AddOutputFilterByType DEFLATE text/html

AddOutputFilterByType DEFLATE text/css

AddOutputFilterByType DEFLATE text/javascript

</IfModule>

Example (HTML):
<img src="image.jpg" loading="lazy" alt="Lazy-loaded image">

By implementing these site speed optimization techniques, you can enhance user experience, boost search engine rankings, and ultimately drive more organic traffic to your website. Regularly monitor your site's performance using tools like Google PageSpeed Insights, GTmetrix, or Pingdom to identify and address speed-related issues.

STRUCTURED DATA MARKUP

Enhancing Website Visibility with Structured Data Markup

When it comes to dominating search engines and gaining a competitive edge in the online world, harnessing the power of structured data markup is an essential step. In this chapter, we will delve into the intricacies of implementing schema markup, rich snippets, and other structured data elements to enhance your website's visibility in search results. By providing search engines with valuable information about your content, you can optimize your website's performance and take your SEO strategies to the next level.

Section 1: Understanding Structured Data Markup

To truly grasp the potential of structured data markup, it is crucial to understand what it is and how it works. Structured data refers to the organization of information in a specific format, making it easier for search engines to interpret and display relevant data to users. By implementing structured data markup, you can provide search engines with context about your content and enable them to display rich snippets – brief summaries containing key information – in search results.

1.1 What is Schema Markup?

Schema markup is a specific vocabulary or code that you can add to your website's HTML to enhance the way search engines read and understand your content. It acts as a common language between search engines and website owners, improving the visibility of search results by providing additional information about your content. Schema markup enables search engines to display rich snippets, such as review ratings, event dates, product prices, and more, directly in search results, offering users a preview of what they can expect from your website.

1.2 The Importance of Structured Data Elements

Alongside schema markup, there are various structured data elements that you can implement on your website to provide search engines with even more valuable information. These elements include, but are not limited to:

1.2.1 Breadcrumbs

Breadcrumbs are navigational elements that provide users and search engines with a clear hierarchy of the pages on your website. By implementing breadcrumbs, you can make it easier for users to navigate your website and understand its structure, while also improving search engines' understanding of your content. Breadcrumbs can enhance the user experience and increase your website's visibility in search results.

1.2.2 FAQ Pages

Implementing Frequently Asked Questions (FAQ) pages on your website can significantly improve your visibility in search results. By structuring your FAQs using schema markup, you can enable search engines to display individual questions and answers directly in search results, increasing the chances of attracting organic traffic and earning featured snippets.

1.2.3 Local Business Information

For businesses with physical locations, structured data markup can be used to provide detailed information about your business, such as its address, opening hours, contact details, and customer reviews. By implementing structured data for local business information, you can increase your chances of appearing in local search results, attracting nearby customers, and boosting your online presence.

1.2.4 Product Markup

For e-commerce websites, implementing structured data markup for products is crucial. By providing search engines with detailed information about your products, such as their price, availability, customer reviews, and more, you can enhance the visibility of your products in search results and increase the likelihood of attracting potential customers.

Section 2: Implementing Structured Data Markup Effectively

Now that we understand the importance of structured data markup and its various elements, it's time to explore how to implement it effectively on your website. By following these steps, you can ensure that your structured data markup is implemented correctly, positively impacting your website's visibility in search results.

2.1 Research and Choose the Right Schema Markup

Before implementing structured data markup, it is essential to research and choose the right schema markup for your content. Schema.org provides a comprehensive list of schemas that cover various industries and types of content, such as articles, reviews, recipes, events, and more. By selecting the most relevant schema markup for your website's content, you can provide search engines with accurate information and increase the chances of appearing in applicable search results.

2.2 Embed the Schema Markup on Your Website

To embed schema markup on your website, you need to add the appropriate structured data elements to your website's HTML. This can be done manually by adding the schema markup code directly to your website's existing HTML code or through the use of plugins or tools specifically designed for schema markup implementation. Whichever method you choose, it is crucial to ensure that the schema markup is added correctly and validated to avoid any potential issues.

2.3 Test and Validate Your Structured Data Markup

Once you have embedded the schema markup on your website, it is essential to test and validate it to ensure its effectiveness. Google's Structured Data Testing Tool allows you to check if your structured data elements are implemented correctly and if any errors or warnings need to be addressed. Regularly testing and validating your schema markup will help you identify any issues and make necessary adjustments to optimize your website's visibility in search results.

2.4 Monitor and Maintain Your Structured Data Markup

Structured data markup is not a one-time implementation. To ensure its continued effectiveness, it is crucial to monitor and maintain your schema markup regularly. As search engines evolve and update their algorithms, it is essential to stay up-to-date with any changes or new recommendations related to structured data markup. By keeping an eye on the performance of your structured data markup and staying informed about any updates, you can maintain and enhance your website's visibility in search results.

2.5 Leverage Enhanced Search Display Features

Implementing structured data markup not only improves your website's visibility in search results but also unlocks additional search display features. Utilizing these enhanced search display features can significantly impact your website's click-through rate and attract more organic traffic. For example, by implementing product markup, you can enable search engines to display products with their prices, reviews, and availability directly in search results, making it easier for users to make informed decisions and increasing the chances of converting them into customers.

Recap:

In this chapter, we explored the world of structured data markup and how it can enhance your website's visibility in search results. By implementing schema markup, rich snippets, and other structured data elements, you provide search engines with valuable information about your content, making it easier for them to understand and display relevant data to users. From understanding the importance of schema markup to implementing it effectively and leveraging enhanced search display features, you now have the tools and knowledge to take your website's SEO strategies to new heights. Harness the power of structured data markup and unlock the full potential of your website's visibility in search results.

Structured data markup, often implemented using schema.org vocabulary, is essential for search engine optimization (SEO). It helps search engines understand the content of web pages better, leading to more accurate and informative search results. Here's a breakdown of structured data markup by SEO importance, along with brief examples:

1. **Rich Snippets**:

- Rich snippets provide additional information in search results, increasing click-through rates.
- Example: Adding schema markup for a recipe with details like cooking time, calories, and user reviews.

```
<script type="application/ld+json">
{
  "@context": "http://schema.org",
  "@type": "Recipe",
  "name": "Homemade Pizza",
  "prepTime": "PT30M",
  "cookTime": "PT20M",
  "nutrition": {
    "@type": "NutritionInformation",
    "calories": "285 calories"
  },
  "aggregateRating": {
    "@type": "AggregateRating",
    "ratingValue": "4.9",
    "reviewCount": "35"
  }
}
</script>
```

Breadcrumbs:

```
<script type="application/ld+json">
{
  "@context": "http://schema.org",
  "@type": "BreadcrumbList",
  "itemListElement": [
    {
      "@type": "ListItem",
```

```
    "position": 1,
    "item": {
      "@id": "https://example.com",
      "name": "Home"
    }
  },
  {
    "@type": "ListItem",
    "position": 2,
    "item": {
      "@id": "https://example.com/products",
      "name": "Products"
    }
  }
]
}
</script> } </script>
```

2. **Local Business**:

```
<script type="application/ld+json">
{
  "@context": "http://schema.org",
  "@type": "Restaurant",
  "name": "Gourmet Bistro",
  "address": {
    "@type": "PostalAddress",
    "streetAddress": "123 Main St",
    "addressLocality": "Anytown",
    "addressRegion": "CA",
    "postalCode": "12345"
  },
  "telephone": "+1-555-123-4567",
  "priceRange": "$$",
  "servesCuisine": "French, Italian"
}
```

```
</script>
```

3. **Product**:
4. **FAQ Page**:
   - FAQ markup can lead to rich search results with expanded question-and-answer sections.

```
} </script>
```

Remember to use structured data markup responsibly, accurately, and in accordance with schema.org guidelines. Properly implemented structured data can improve the visibility of your content in search results and enhance the user experience.

MOBILE OPTIMIZATION

Hello, fellow SEO enthusiasts! Welcome to the next chapter of our book, where we delve into the world of mobile optimization. In this digital age, where almost everyone uses smartphones and tablets, it has become imperative for businesses to optimize their websites for mobile devices. Not only does this ensure a seamless user experience, but it also has a significant impact on search engine rankings.

As an SEO expert, I have witnessed first-hand the immense value of mobile optimization. In this chapter, I will walk you through the step-by-step process of optimizing your website for mobile devices, as well as dive into the various techniques and best practices for effective mobile optimization. So, let's get started!

STEP 1:

RESPONSIVE DESIGN

The first and perhaps the most crucial step in mobile optimization is implementing a responsive design. With responsive design, your website will automatically adapt to the screen size of the device it is being accessed on. Whether it is a smartphone, tablet, or desktop computer, your website will provide an optimal viewing experience for users.

To achieve this, you need to ensure that your

website layout, images, and content are all flexible and adjust according to the screen size. This eliminates the need for creating separate mobile versions of your website and makes it easier to manage your content. Responsive design not only enhances the user experience but also helps improve your search engine rankings.

STEP 2:

MOBILE-
FRIENDLY
NAVIGATION

O nce you have implemented a responsive design, the next step is to optimize your website's navigation for mobile devices. While navigation on a desktop website is usually done through a navigation bar at the top, this might not work well on a mobile device due to limited screen space.

To create a mobile-friendly navigation, consider using a hamburger menu, which is a collapsible menu icon that expands when clicked, revealing the navigation options. This allows users to access the menu without cluttering the screen. Additionally, make sure your navigation links and buttons are large enough to be easily clickable on a smaller touch screen.

STEP 3:

SITE SPEED OPTIMIZATION

I n today's fast-paced world, no one has the patience to wait for a slow-loading website. This applies even more so when it comes to browsing on mobile devices. Therefore, optimizing your website's speed is essential for a seamless user experience and higher search engine rankings.

To improve your site speed, consider compressing images to reduce file size without compromising quality. Minify your HTML, CSS, and JavaScript files to eliminate unnecessary characters and reduce load times. Leverage browser caching to store static elements of your website, reducing the need for recurrent downloads. Additionally, use a content delivery network (CDN) to ensure faster loading times for users across different geographical locations.

STEP 4:

MOBILE OPTIMIZATION BEST PRACTICES

In addition to the above steps, here are some best practices you should follow to maximize your website's mobile optimization:

1. Optimize your meta tags: Ensure your title tags and meta descriptions are concise, compelling, and relevant to the page content. This helps search

engines understand the context of your website and improves click-through rates.

2. Use responsive images: Resize and compress images to fit different screen sizes without compromising quality. This helps reduce load times and ensures a visually appealing experience for mobile users.

3. Prioritize mobile content: Mobile users often have different needs and behaviors compared to desktop users. Make sure your website's content is optimized for mobile devices, with clear and concise headings, easy-to-read fonts, and shorter paragraphs.

4. Implement mobile-friendly forms: If your website includes forms, ensure they are designed to be easily filled out on a mobile device. Use dropdown menus, checkboxes, and radio buttons to simplify the process, and minimize the number of required fields.

Conclusion:

Congratulations! You have now taken significant steps towards mastering mobile optimization. By implementing a responsive design, optimizing your website's navigation, improving site speed, and following mobile optimization best practices, you are well on your way to delivering a seamless mobile experience to your users and boosting your search engine rankings.

Remember, the mobile landscape is continually evolving, and it is crucial to stay updated with the latest trends and technologies. Regularly monitor your website's performance on mobile devices, conduct user testing, and adapt your optimization strategies accordingly. By doing so, you are sure to dominate search engines and leave your competitors in awe of your mobile optimization prowess.

Mobile optimization is crucial for SEO (Search Engine Optimization) as search engines like Google prioritize mobile-friendly websites in their rankings. With the increasing use of smartphones for web browsing, ensuring a positive mobile user experience is essential for your website's visibility and success. Here are some important aspects of mobile optimization along with brief examples:

1. **Responsive Web Design**:
2. **Page Speed**:
3. **Mobile-First Indexing**:
4. **Mobile-Friendly Content**:
5. **Touch-Friendly Design**:

6. **Optimized Images and Videos**:
7. **Minimize Pop-Ups and Interstitials**:
8. **Mobile SEO-Friendly URLs**:
9. **Structured Data Markup**:
10. **Mobile-Friendly Testing**:

Keep up the excellent work, and I'll see you in the next chapter!

5

LOCAL SEO DOMINATION

THE IMPORTANCE OF LOCAL SEO

I n this chapter, I will guide you through the step-by-step process of mastering local SEO. We will delve into why it is essential for businesses with a physical presence, explore the benefits of local search, and provide strategies to optimize your website and online presence to dominate search engines locally.

First and foremost, it is important to understand why local SEO is crucial for businesses with a physical presence. While traditional advertising methods such as print ads and word-of-mouth still have their place, the majority of consumers now turn to search engines to find local businesses. Whether it's searching for a nearby restaurant, a local pet store, or a specific service provider, people rely on search engines like Google to provide them with the most relevant and accurate results.

Think about it: when was the last time you searched for a business's phone number in the Yellow Pages? Chances are, you can't even remember. That's because search engine optimization has revolutionized the way we search for products and services. It has made the process quicker, more efficient, and more personalized.

Now, let's move on to the benefits of local search. When you optimize your website and online presence for local search, you are putting your business in front of potential customers at the exact moment they are actively looking for what you offer. This targeted approach significantly increases the likelihood of attracting highly qualified leads and converting them into paying customers.

Furthermore, local search has a higher conversion rate compared to other online marketing channels. According to recent studies, 78% of local mobile searches result in offline purchases. This statistic alone highlights the tremendous potential local SEO has in driving customers to your physical store and increasing your revenue.

Additionally, local search optimization helps you establish a strong local online presence, which in turn builds credibility and trust with your target audience. When your business appears at the top of search engine results pages (SERPs) consistently, it sends a message to potential customers that you are a reputable and trustworthy company. This can give you a competitive edge over your competitors, especially in highly saturated markets.

Now, let me guide you through the step-by-step process of mastering local SEO. The first step is to optimize your website for local search. This involves creating and optimizing landing pages specifically tailored to each location you serve. For example, if you have multiple store locations, you should create individual landing pages for each location and optimize them with location-specific keywords, content, and metadata.

Next, it's crucial to claim and optimize your Google My Business listing. Google My Business is a free tool that allows businesses to manage their online presence across Google, including Search and Maps. By claiming your listing and ensuring that all information is accurate and up to date, you increase your chances of appearing in the coveted Google local pack, which is the top section of local search results that showcases local businesses.

Another important aspect of local SEO is building citations. Citations are online mentions of your business's name, address, and phone number (NAP) on various directories, maps, and review sites. These citations help search engines validate the information about your business and establish trust. You should aim to build consistent and accurate citations on reputable directories such as Yelp, Yellow Pages, and industry-specific directories.

Furthermore, online reviews play a significant role in local SEO. Positive reviews not only help build trust with potential customers but also improve your search engine rankings. Encourage satisfied customers to leave reviews on platforms such as Google My Business, Yelp, and Facebook. Responding to reviews, whether positive or negative, shows that you value customer feedback and are committed to providing excellent service.

Lastly, don't underestimate the power of local link building. Identify local websites, blogs, and organizations that are relevant to your business and reach out to them for potential partnerships, guest posts, or backlink opportunities. These local backlinks not only drive traffic to your website but also signal to search engines that your business is local and relevant to the community.

By following these step-by-step strategies, you can dominate local search and ensure that your business stands out from the competition. Remember, local SEO isn't just about appearing in search engine results; it's about attracting local customers, increasing store visits, and establishing a strong local online presence. So, take the time to optimize your website, claim your Google My Business listing, build citations and online reviews, and engage in local link building. Embrace the power of local SEO, and watch your business thrive in the digital age.

GOOGLE MY BUSINESS OPTIMIZATION

Introduction:

In the ever-evolving digital landscape, businesses are constantly seeking new ways to optimize their online presence. While traditional SEO techniques are crucial, focusing on local search results through Google My Business has emerged as a game-changer. In this chapter, I will guide you through the process of creating and optimizing your Google My Business listing, managing customer reviews, and harnessing the full potential of this powerful local SEO tool.

Section 1: Creating Your Google My Business Listing

1.1 Getting Started:

To embark on your journey towards enhanced local visibility, the first step is to create a Google My Business listing. This can be done by visiting the Google My Business website and signing in with your Google account. Once you've logged in, you'll be prompted to provide essential details about your business, such as its name, address, phone number, and category. Accuracy and consistency are key here, as any discrepancies can negatively impact your search ranking.

1.2 Providing Detailed Information:

Beyond the basic contact details, make sure to furnish your listing with comprehensive and accurate information about your business. This includes your hours of operation, website URL, and a description that highlights what sets your business apart. Adding enticing photos and videos can further capture the attention of potential customers, boosting engagement and credibility.

1.3 Choosing the Right Category:

Selecting the most relevant and specific category for your business is crucial for improved visibility. Google provides a wide range of categories to choose from, ensuring that your listing aligns with users' search queries accurately. This step is often overlooked but can significantly impact your ranking in local searches.

Section 2: Optimizing Your Google My Business Listing

2.1 Keyword Research:

Keyword research is a foundational aspect of any SEO strategy, and optimizing your Google My Business listing is no exception. Conduct thorough research to identify relevant keywords that potential customers are using in local searches. Incorporate these keywords into your listing's description, ensuring a seamless integration that feels natural and informative.

2.2 Google Posts:

Google Posts enable you to engage directly with your target audience through your Google My Business listing. Craft engaging and informative posts that provide value to your audience, showcasing your expertise and announcing special offers. These posts are visible in search results, further promoting your business and encouraging click-throughs.

2.3 Utilizing Attributes:

Attributes are additional details that can be

added to your Google My Business listing, providing potential customers with more specific information about what sets your business apart. These attributes can include features like wheelchair accessibility, outdoor seating, Wi-Fi availability, and more. By taking full advantage of these attributes, you increase the chances of your listing appearing in specific local searches catered to users' preferences.

Section 3: Managing Customer Reviews

3.1 Encouraging Reviews:

Customer reviews play a significant role in shaping the perception of your business. Actively encourage satisfied customers to leave reviews on your Google My Business listing by promoting it through your website, social media channels, and in-store promotions. The more positive reviews you amass, the stronger your online reputation will become, attracting more customers and boosting your ranking in local search results.

3.2 Responding to Reviews:

Managing customer reviews involves not only promoting the positive but also addressing any negative feedback. Take the time to respond to each review, whether positive or negative. Show gratitude and appreciation for positive reviews, and offer a genuine and respectful response to negative ones. This demonstrates your commitment to customer satisfaction and portrays your business as proactive and attentive.

3.3 Leveraging Reviews as Social Proof:

Customer reviews can serve as powerful social proof for your business. Highlight positive reviews on your website, social media profiles, and other marketing materials, showcasing the experiences of satisfied customers. This not only enhances your credibility but also encourages potential customers to choose your business over competitors.

Section 4: Utilizing Google My Business as a Local SEO Tool

4.1 Insights and Analytics:

Google My Business provides valuable insights and analytics data that can help you understand your customers' behavior and preferences better. Monitor these metrics regularly to gain insights into how customers are finding and engaging with your listing, enabling you to fine-tune your local SEO strategies accordingly.

4.2 Tracking Competitors:

Stay aware of your competitors' activities by monitoring their Google My Business listings. Observe the keywords they are targeting, the offers they are promoting, and any changes they make to their listing. This competitive intelligence can inform your own local SEO efforts, allowing you to stay one step ahead in the local search results.

Conclusion:

Optimizing your Google My Business listing is a powerful strategy for maximizing your visibility in local search results. By following the step-by-step guide provided in this chapter, you can create a compelling and informative listing, effectively manage customer reviews, and harness the full potential of Google My Business as a local SEO tool. Embrace the power of Google My Business optimization, and watch your business soar to new heights in the digital realm.

Local SEO Domination refers to the strategies and techniques used to maximize a business's visibility in local search engine results. This is crucial for attracting customers in a specific geographical area. Here's a breakdown of key aspects of Local SEO importance with brief examples:

1. **Google My Business (GMB) Optimization**:
2. **Keyword Research and Targeting**:
3. **On-Page SEO**:
4. **Local Citations and NAP Consistency**:
5. **Local Link Building**:

6. **Online Reviews and Ratings**:
7. **Mobile Optimization**:
8. **Schema Markup**:
9. **Local Content Creation**:
10. **Social Media Presence**:

LOCAL CITATIONS AND NAP CONSISTENCY

When it comes to local SEO, a key factor that can greatly impact your online visibility is local citations and NAP consistency. In this chapter, we will delve into the details of why these elements are crucial for dominating search engines in your local market. I will also share step-by-step strategies on how to build citations, ensure NAP consistency across online directories, and ultimately improve your local search rankings.

Section 1: Understanding the Importance of Local Citations

Before we dive into the nitty-gritty of local

citations and NAP consistency, it's essential to understand what exactly they are and why they matter in the realm of search engine optimization.

Local citations refer to references of your business's Name, Address, and Phone Number (NAP) on other websites, directories, and online platforms. These references can include your business name, address, phone number, website URL, and even additional information like business hours, reviews, and photos.

Citations serve as trust signals for search engines, helping them verify the legitimacy and relevance of your business. When search engines see consistent citations across various platforms, they gain confidence in displaying your business in local search results, driving more organic traffic to your website.

Section 2: Building Local Citations for SEO Success

Now that we understand the significance of local citations, let's dive into the step-by-step process of building them effectively to boost your local search rankings.

STEP 1:

CONDUCT A CITATIONS AUDIT

Start by conducting a thorough audit of your existing local citations. This means searching for your business name, address, and phone number across different online directories, social media platforms, and review sites. Make a list of all the websites where your business is mentioned and analyze the accuracy, consistency, and completeness of the NAP information.

STEP 2:

PRIORITIZE POPULAR DIRECTORIES

Research and identify the most influential and relevant online directories in your industry or location. These directories often have high domain authority and a significant local user base. Focus on building citations on these platforms to maximize your visibility and generate quality leads.

STEP 3:

CLAIM AND OPTIMIZE YOUR GOOGLE MY BUSINESS LISTING

One of the most critical citations for local SEO is your Google My Business (GMB) listing. Start by claiming and verifying your GMB profile. Ensure that your NAP information is accurate, complete, and consistent with the information on your website. Optimize your GMB listing by adding relevant categories, business descriptions, high-quality images, and customer reviews.

STEP 4:

LEVERAGE INDUSTRY-SPECIFIC DIRECTORIES

I n addition to popular general directories, explore industry-specific directories that cater to your niche. These directories can provide targeted exposure to potential customers searching for businesses like yours. Examples include healthcare directories, restaurant directories, and professional service directories.

STEP 5:

ENCOURAGE USER REVIEWS

Positive customer reviews can greatly boost your local search rankings. Encourage your satisfied customers to leave reviews on your Google My Business listing, social media platforms, and popular review sites. Respond to all reviews, whether positive or negative, to demonstrate a strong online presence and commitment to customer satisfaction.

Section 3: Ensuring NAP Consistency Across Online Directories

While building citations is crucial, maintaining

NAP consistency across online directories is equally important. Inconsistent NAP information can confuse search engines and harm your local search rankings. Follow the step-by-step strategies below to ensure NAP consistency across all your citations.

STEP 1:

CREATE A MASTER NAP PROFILE

C reate a master NAP profile that serves as a reference for all your online citations. This profile should include your business name, exact address (including suite numbers or unit numbers if applicable), and a consistent phone number format. Ensure that this information matches the details on your official

website.

STEP 2:

UPDATE EXISTING CITATIONS

Using the master NAP profile, update any existing citations where the information is inaccurate or inconsistent. This may involve contacting directory owners or using citation management tools to streamline the process. Keep track of the directories you have updated to ensure no inconsistencies remain.

STEP 3:

MONITOR NEW CITATIONS

Regularly monitor for new citations that may pop up, both intentionally and unintentionally. Set up Google Alerts or use citation monitoring tools to receive alerts whenever your business is mentioned online. If you come across new citations with inconsistent NAP information, take immediate action to correct them.

STEP 4:

COMMUNICATE NAP CONSISTENCY GUIDELINES

If you have employees or franchisees who manage local SEO for different locations, it is crucial to communicate NAP consistency guidelines. Provide clear instructions on how to handle citations and ensure they always refer to the master NAP profile.

Section 4: Improving Local Search Rankings with Local Citations and NAP Consistency

Now that you've built local citations and ensured NAP consistency, it's time to reap the rewards of improved local search rankings. Here are some additional strategies to enhance your local SEO efforts.

Strategy 1: Monitor and Respond to Reviews

Regularly monitor online reviews and respond promptly and professionally. Engaging with customers shows your commitment to their satisfaction, builds trust, and can positively impact your local search rankings.

Strategy 2: Implement Schema Markup

Implementing schema markup on your website can provide search engines with structured data about your business, including your NAP details. This helps search engines understand and display your business information accurately in local search results.

Strategy 3: Optimize Your Website For Local Keywords

Research and incorporate relevant local keywords throughout your website, including in your content, page titles, meta descriptions, and header tags. Optimizing your website with local keywords can increase its relevance in local search results.

By understanding the importance of local citations and NAP consistency in local SEO and implementing the strategies outlined above, you'll be well on your way to dominating search engines in your local market. Remember, consistency is key, so regularly monitor and update your citations to maintain a strong online presence. Take control of your local search rankings and drive more organic traffic to your business with the power of local citations and NAP consistency.

6

ADAPTING TO ALGORITHM UPDATES

The Ever-Evolving World of
Search Engine Algorithms

Search engines are constantly evolving to enhance user experience and deliver more relevant and high-quality results. To achieve this, search engines like Google, Bing, and Yahoo regularly introduce algorithm updates that refine their ranking criteria. These updates are aimed at weeding out spammy websites, rewarding valuable content, and providing users with the best possible search experience.

Algorithm updates come in various forms and sizes. Some are minor adjustments that go unnoticed, while others are massive overhauls that send shockwaves through the SEO community. The impact of algorithm updates can be substantial, causing fluctuations in rankings and website traffic. As an SEO professional, it is crucial to stay updated on algorithm changes and understand their implications for your website.

Interpreting Algorithm Changes:

Interpreting algorithm changes is like decoding a complex puzzle. When a new update is rolled out, it can be challenging to pinpoint the exact changes and how they affect your website. However, with the right approach, you can unravel the mystery and gain valuable insights.

One strategy to decipher algorithm changes is to closely monitor your website's performance metrics. Keep a close eye on your rankings, organic search traffic, conversion rates, and user engagement metrics. Any sudden fluctuations can be an indicator of an algorithm update. By analyzing these changes and comparing them to the timing of known algorithm updates, you can start to understand the impact of the update on your website.

Another valuable source of information is professional SEO communities and forums. Engaging with fellow SEO professionals and discussing algorithm updates can provide you with different perspectives and insights. It is essential to participate in these conversations, share your experiences, and learn from others' knowledge. After all, the SEO community is a collective powerhouse of expertise, and working together can uncover answers that may elude you individually.

Adapting Your SEO Strategy Accordingly:

Once you have identified and interpreted an algorithm update, the next crucial step is adapting your SEO strategy accordingly. Algorithm updates often reflect a shift in search engine priorities, and your strategy must align with these changes to maintain visibility and rankings.

First and foremost, it is essential to evaluate your website's content. With each algorithm update, search engines are getting better at understanding the context and intent behind search queries. This means that high-quality, relevant, and insightful content is becoming paramount. Conduct a thorough audit of your content, ensuring it meets the highest standards of quality, relevance, and usefulness to searchers. Update and optimize your content to align with the latest algorithm changes and user expectations.

In addition to content, you must also focus on technical aspects of your website. Search engines prefer websites that are fast, secure, and mobile-friendly. Ensure your website is optimized for speed by compressing images, minifying code, and implementing caching techniques. Address any security issues, such as updating SSL certificates and protecting against malware. Finally, make sure your website is fully responsive and user-friendly on all devices. These technical aspects are critical for both user experience and search engine rankings.

It is also crucial to consider user experience as a key component of your SEO strategy. Search engines are increasingly using user signals like bounce rate, time on page, and click-through rates to evaluate website quality. Optimizing your website for a seamless user experience can positively impact your rankings. Pay attention to factors such as site navigation, internal linking, readability, and overall user engagement. By providing a highly usable and enjoyable experience, you are more likely to earn favorable rankings in the post-algorithm update landscape.

Mitigating the Risks of Algorithmic Penalties:

While algorithm updates are intended to improve search quality, they can also subject websites to algorithmic penalties. These penalties can be detrimental to your visibility and rankings, and it is essential to mitigate the risks associated with them.

One way to mitigate algorithmic penalties is to adhere to search engine guidelines and best practices. Ensure that your website follows ethical SEO techniques and avoids any questionable practices that might be penalized. Keep a close watch on your backlink profile, ensuring it is natural, diverse, and of high quality. Remove or disavow any low-quality or spammy backlinks that could potentially harm your rankings.

Regularly monitor your website for potential issues and promptly address any technical or content-related problems. Conduct regular audits to identify and fix any broken links, duplicate content, or thin pages. By proactively maintaining your website's health and relevance, you reduce the chances of algorithmic penalties and increase your chances of ranking well.

Conclusion:

Understanding algorithm updates is an essential skill in the world of SEO. By gaining insights into algorithm changes, interpreting their impact, and adapting your SEO strategy accordingly, you can navigate the ever-changing digital landscape with confidence. Remember that algorithm updates are not meant to be your adversary but an opportunity to improve and showcase your website's value. Embrace the challenge, stay informed, and continuously evolve your SEO strategies to dominate the search engine rankings.

Building a Resilient SEO Strategy

As I delve into the intricacies of search engine optimization, I realize the importance of building a strategy that can withstand the ever-evolving world of algorithms and ensure long-term visibility. In this chapter, I will guide you through the process of constructing a resilient SEO strategy that not only helps your website maintain a strong presence in search engine results but also diversifies your traffic sources, builds a robust brand presence, and prioritizes the user experience.

1. Understanding Algorithm Updates

Before we can build a resilient SEO strategy, it is vital to comprehend the impact and significance of algorithm updates. Search engines like Google constantly refine their algorithms to provide users with the most relevant and high-quality search results. As an SEO practitioner, staying abreast of these updates ensures that you can navigate through algorithmic changes while maintaining your visibility in search engine results.

One effective way to stay informed about algorithm updates is by following reputable SEO news sources, attending industry conferences, and engaging in communities where professionals share insights and experiences. By staying ahead of the curve, you can respond to algorithm updates proactively rather than reactively, ensuring that your SEO strategy remains resilient throughout.

2. Diversify Your Traffic Sources

Relying solely on organic search traffic can be risky in the ever-changing world of SEO. To develop a resilient SEO strategy, it is essential to diversify your traffic sources, reducing your dependency on search engines alone. By expanding your reach across different channels, you can safeguard your online presence and mitigate the impact of algorithm updates.

One way to diversify your traffic sources is by investing in paid advertising campaigns. Platforms like Google Ads and social media ads allow you to target specific audiences, reach new users, and drive traffic to your website even when organic search rankings fluctuate. Additionally, you can leverage email marketing, social media marketing, and content syndication to tap into different sources of traffic and increase your overall visibility.

3. Building a Strong Brand Presence

A resilient SEO strategy goes beyond focusing solely on keywords and search rankings. It also involves establishing a strong brand presence that resonates with your target audience. By building a recognizable and trustworthy brand, you can develop a sustainable SEO strategy that can withstand algorithm updates.

To build a strong brand presence, start by defining your brand's identity and values. This involves understanding your target audience, creating a unique brand voice, and consistently delivering high-quality content and services that align with your brand promise. By doing so, you can foster brand loyalty, encourage brand mentions, and attract natural backlinks, all of which contribute to long-term visibility in search engine results.

4. Prioritizing User Experience

In the world of SEO, user experience has become a crucial factor in determining search engine rankings. Search engines now prioritize websites that provide a seamless and enjoyable user experience, rewarding them with higher visibility in search results. Therefore, developing a resilient SEO strategy involves prioritizing user experience across all aspects of your website.

Begin by ensuring that your website is fast, responsive, and mobile-friendly. Page loading speed and mobile compatibility are critical factors that affect user experience and search engine rankings alike. In addition, create an intuitive navigation structure, optimize your website's architecture, and make your content easily accessible and digestible. By providing a user-friendly experience, you not only improve your chances of ranking well in search engine results but also increase engagement and conversions.

5. Evolving with SEO Trends

Building a resilient SEO strategy requires adaptability and a willingness to evolve with the ever-changing SEO landscape. What works today may not necessarily work tomorrow, as algorithms continue to evolve and user behaviors change. Therefore, it is crucial to continually monitor SEO trends and refine your strategy accordingly.

Stay updated with emerging SEO techniques and best practices by reading industry-leading blogs, participating in relevant forums, and attending SEO conferences. Experiment with new strategies, track their effectiveness, and adapt accordingly. By constantly evolving, testing, and refining your SEO approach, you ensure that your strategy remains resilient in the face of algorithm updates and changing search engine dynamics.

In conclusion, developing a resilient SEO strategy is crucial for effectively dominating search engines and maintaining long-term visibility. By understanding algorithm updates, diversifying traffic sources, building a strong brand presence, prioritizing user experience, and adapting to SEO trends, you can construct a strategy that withstands the test of time. Stay proactive, remain adaptable, and let your SEO mastery lead your website to new heights of success.

Staying Ahead of the Curve

As I sit here, pondering the ever-evolving world of SEO, I can't help but marvel at the immense opportunities and challenges it presents. Being an SEO practitioner myself, I've come to understand that staying ahead of the curve is not just a desire; it is a necessity. In this chapter, I will share with you my insights and strategies for mastering the art of staying ahead in the dynamic landscape of search engine optimization.

Section 1: Emerging Trends in SEO

The first step to staying ahead of the curve is to be aware of the emerging trends in SEO. Keeping a finger on the pulse of the industry allows you to anticipate changes and adapt your strategies accordingly. One key trend that has been gaining traction is voice search. With the rise of virtual assistants like Alexa and Siri, optimizing your website for voice search is becoming increasingly important. Understanding how users interact with these technologies and tailoring your content to match their conversational queries will set you apart from your competitors.

Another trend to watch out for is the increasing emphasis on user experience (UX). Search engines are constantly refining their algorithms to prioritize websites that provide a seamless and enjoyable user experience. This means that factors such as page speed, mobile-friendliness, and intuitive navigation are crucial for SEO success. Keep up with the latest UX best practices and make sure your website delivers an exceptional user experience across all devices.

Section 2: Innovative Strategies for SEO Excellence

In addition to being aware of emerging trends, it's important to implement innovative strategies that give you an edge over your competitors. One such strategy is the optimization of featured snippets. Featured snippets are the concise answer boxes that appear at the top of search engine results pages (SERPs). By optimizing your content to appear as a featured snippet, you can increase your website's visibility and drive more organic traffic. Structuring your content in a way that directly answers common user queries and using schema markup to provide more context to search engines are some effective techniques for capturing featured snippets.

Another strategy that sets you apart from the competition is the use of long-tail keywords. While short keywords are highly competitive, long-tail keywords are more specific, targeted, and less competitive. By focusing on long-tail keywords that are relevant to your niche, you can attract highly qualified traffic that is more likely to convert. Conduct thorough keyword research and create high-quality, informative content around these long-tail keywords to reap the benefits of this strategy.

Section 3: Industry Insights and the Power of Networking

Understanding the dynamics of the SEO industry is essential for staying ahead of the curve. Attending industry conferences, webinars, and workshops not only provides you with valuable insights and knowledge but also allows you to network with like-minded professionals. Building relationships with industry experts and fellow practitioners gives you access to insider information, case studies, and collaborative opportunities. Surround yourself with individuals who share your passion for SEO and forge meaningful connections that will foster your growth and keep you ahead of the curve.

Additionally, staying updated with industry news and publications is vital. Subscribe to reputable SEO blogs and newsletters, follow industry leaders on social media, and actively participate in relevant online forums. By immersing yourself in the SEO community, you can stay informed about the latest trends, algorithm updates, and best practices. Embrace a continuous learning mindset and commit to staying up-to-date with the ever-changing SEO landscape.

Section 4: Adaptation and Agility as Key Competencies

Lastly, it's important to cultivate adaptability and agility as core competencies in the fast-paced world of SEO. In an industry where algorithms and best practices can change overnight, being able to adapt quickly and pivot your strategies is crucial for success. Monitor your website's performance regularly, conduct frequent audits, and analyze data to identify areas of improvement. Utilize analytics tools to gain insights into user behavior and adjust your SEO strategies accordingly. Don't be afraid to experiment, test new techniques, and iterate based on the results. Embracing an adaptable mindset ensures that you are always one step ahead of the curve.

Conclusion:

As we conclude this chapter on staying ahead of the curve in SEO, I hope you have gained valuable insights and strategies to propel yourself towards SEO excellence. Remember to stay aware of emerging trends, implement innovative strategies, seek industry insights, and cultivate adaptability and agility. By continuously learning and evolving, you can establish yourself as a master of SEO and thrive in the ever-evolving world of search engine domination. Keep your finger on the pulse of the industry, push the boundaries of innovation, and be relentless in your pursuit of SEO mastery.

Adapting to these changes is crucial for maintaining and improving your website's SEO. Here's a guide on how to do it with brief examples:

7

MEASURING SEO SUCCESS

Setting SEO Goals and KPIs

As I ventured further into the complex world of SEO, I learned that success in this field requires a well-defined set of goals and key performance indicators (KPIs). These measurements would not only gauge our progress but also help align our efforts with our overarching business objectives. So today, I want to share with you the importance of defining clear SEO goals and KPIs, as well as guide you through the process of setting realistic targets and tracking your progress.

Without a doubt, the first step in this journey is to establish your SEO goals. This involves identifying what you ultimately want to achieve through your SEO efforts. Is it to increase organic traffic to your website? Improve your search engine rankings? Attract more potential customers? Or perhaps establish yourself as a thought leader in your industry? Take some time to reflect on your unique business needs and aspirations, as these will shape the goals you set.

Once you have a clear sense of your objectives, it's important to break them down into smaller, achievable targets. These targets will serve as milestones along the way, allowing you to track your progress and make any necessary adjustments. For instance, if your overall goal is to increase organic traffic by 50% within the next six months, you can set monthly targets to ensure you're on track. Remember, each goal should be specific, measurable, attainable, relevant, and time-bound (SMART). This framework will help you stay focused and motivated throughout your SEO journey.

Next, let's talk about key performance indicators (KPIs). These metrics act as quantitative measurements of your progress towards your goals. By tracking KPIs, you can assess the effectiveness of your SEO strategies and tactics. It's essential to choose KPIs that align with your objectives and provide meaningful insights into your SEO performance. Some common KPIs to consider include organic traffic, search engine rankings, conversion rates, and bounce rates. However, the KPIs you choose will depend on your specific goals and industry.

When setting KPIs, it's crucial to establish baseline measurements. This allows you to benchmark your current performance and track improvements over time. For example, if your current organic traffic is 1000 visitors per month, you can aim to increase it to 1500 visitors per month as your initial KPI. By regularly monitoring these metrics, you can assess the impact of your SEO efforts and identify areas for improvement.

It's important to note that while KPIs provide valuable quantitative data, they don't tell the full story. To achieve a comprehensive understanding of your SEO performance, it's necessary to analyze qualitative factors as well. These qualitative insights can come from user feedback, customer reviews, and surveys. They can reveal valuable information about user experience, user intent, and overall satisfaction with your website. By combining qualitative and quantitative analysis, you'll gain a more holistic view of your SEO performance.

Remember, setting goals and KPIs isn't a one-time task. As your business evolves and your SEO strategies adapt, it's essential to regularly reassess and adjust your goals and KPIs accordingly. The digital landscape is constantly evolving, and your objectives should reflect these changes. Stay up to date with emerging trends and technologies, and be proactive in adjusting your goals to stay ahead of the competition.

Furthermore, it's vital to align your SEO goals and KPIs with your overall business objectives. Your SEO efforts should not be disjointed from the bigger picture. By aligning your SEO goals with your business goals, you can ensure that every action you take contributes to your overall success. For example, if one of your business objectives is to expand into international markets, your SEO goals can focus on improving visibility in specific regions and optimizing for international keywords.

Finally, don't forget the importance of tracking your progress. Regularly reviewing your KPIs and comparing them to your established targets will allow you to measure your success and make informed decisions. Analyze the data, identify trends, and adjust your strategies accordingly. Celebrate your successes and learn from your setbacks. Remember, SEO mastery is an ongoing process, and continuous learning and improvement are key to achieving long-term success.

In conclusion, setting clear SEO goals and KPIs is essential for dominating search engines. By defining your objectives, breaking them down into achievable targets, and tracking your progress through meaningful KPIs, you can align your SEO efforts with your overall business objectives and work towards sustainable success. Remember to constantly reassess and adjust your goals to stay ahead of the competition, and always keep an eye on the evolving digital landscape. With a strategic mindset and a commitment to continuous learning, you'll be well on your way to SEO mastery.

SEO Analytics and Reporting

To start, let's delve into the importance of SEO analytics and reporting. In today's digital landscape, where competition for online visibility is fierce, having access to accurate and reliable data is essential. SEO analytics provide you with the necessary information to evaluate the success of your SEO efforts. It allows you to measure the effectiveness of your strategies, identify areas for improvement, and make data-driven decisions.

When it comes to SEO analytics, there are a plethora of tools available, each offering unique features and functionalities. One of the most popular and powerful analytics tools is Google Analytics. Google Analytics provides you with a wealth of data, allowing you to track website traffic, user behavior, conversions, and much more. By deciphering this data, you can gain deep insights into how users interact with your website, which pages are performing well, and which ones need improvement.

Another tool worth mentioning is Moz Analytics. Moz offers a comprehensive suite of SEO tools, including keyword research, link building, and rank tracking. Moz Analytics allows you to monitor your website's performance, track keyword rankings, and analyze backlink profiles. This data can help you identify potential issues that may be hindering your website's performance in search engine rankings.

SEMrush is yet another powerhouse in the SEO analytics realm. With a robust set of features and functionalities, SEMrush provides you with in-depth competitor analysis, keyword research, and backlink analysis. By analyzing your competitors' strategies, you can gain valuable insights into what works and replicate their success while also identifying gaps in their strategies that you can exploit.

While these tools offer a multitude of benefits, the true value lies in how you analyze and interpret the data they provide. One of the best ways to make sense of the vast amount of data is by creating reports. Reports allow you to organize and present the data in a digestible format, making it easier to understand and draw conclusions from.

When it comes to generating reports, customization is key. Most SEO analytics tools offer pre-built templates that can be tailored to your specific needs. You can choose the metrics you want to include, establish benchmarks and goals, and showcase the data in visually appealing charts and graphs. Customizable reports enable you to highlight the most critical information and present it in a way that resonates with your audience.

Now, let's discuss some key metrics that you should focus on when analyzing SEO data. One of the foundational metrics is organic traffic. Organic traffic refers to the number of visitors that come to your website through search engine results. Monitoring organic traffic allows you to gauge the effectiveness of your SEO efforts over time and track fluctuations in performance. Additionally, organic traffic can be segmented by keywords, landing pages, and geographical locations, providing you with deeper insights into user behavior.

Keyword rankings are another important metric in SEO analytics. By tracking keyword rankings, you can determine how well your website is performing in search engine results for specific keywords. If you notice a drop in rankings, it may indicate that you need to optimize your content or improve your website's overall authority. On the other hand, significant improvements in keyword rankings can be an indication that your SEO strategies are effective and yielding positive results.

Backlink analysis is yet another valuable metric when it comes to SEO analytics. Backlinks are crucial for building authority and credibility in the eyes of search engines. Analyzing your backlink profile allows you to identify high-quality links, assess their impact on your website's performance, and discover new opportunities for link building. Additionally, tracking your competitor's backlink profiles can help you uncover potential link building opportunities and gain a competitive advantage.

Conversion rate optimization (CRO) is a metric that often goes hand in hand with SEO analytics. CRO focuses on improving the percentage of website visitors that take a desired action, such as making a purchase or submitting a contact form. By analyzing user behavior, conducting A/B tests, and implementing strategic changes, you can optimize your website to increase conversion rates. By integrating your SEO analytics with CRO strategies, you can maximize the effectiveness of both and drive tangible results.

In conclusion, exploring the world of SEO analytics and reporting tools is essential to gain valuable insights into your website's performance. Analyzing data, generating reports, and using analytics to optimize your SEO strategy can be a game-changer in the constantly evolving digital landscape. By harnessing the power of SEO analytics, you can stay ahead of the competition, drive meaningful traffic to your website, and ultimately achieve search engine domination. So, it's time to dive deep, explore these cutting-edge tools, and unlock the secrets to SEO success.

Continuous Improvement and Adaptation

Before we delve deeper into the world of continuous improvement and adaptation in SEO, it is imperative to understand the need for such an approach. Search engines, primarily Google, are constantly updating their algorithms to provide the best possible user experience. With each algorithm update, old tactics and techniques may become less effective or even obsolete. Therefore, it is essential to stay on top of these changes and adapt our SEO strategies accordingly.

One of the first steps towards embracing a culture of continuous improvement and adaptation is to constantly test and analyze our SEO efforts. This involves conducting regular audits of our websites to identify any areas that can be optimized further. From on-page elements such as meta tags and keyword density to off-page factors like backlinks and social signals, every aspect of our SEO strategy should be subject to scrutiny.

One effective technique for testing and optimizing your SEO tactics is split testing, also known as A/B testing. This involves creating two or more versions of a webpage or element and measuring the performance of each version. By comparing the results, we can determine which version yields better results and make the necessary adjustments. For example, we can test different headlines, calls-to-action, or even page layouts to see which one resonates better with our target audience.

Another important aspect of continuous improvement and adaptation in SEO is staying updated with industry changes. As I mentioned earlier, search engine algorithms are constantly evolving, and staying ahead of the curve is essential to maintaining a competitive edge. To achieve this, it is vital to keep abreast of the latest industry news, blogs, and forums. Following trusted SEO experts and attending conferences or webinars can also provide valuable insights and keep us up to date with the latest trends and best practices.

Furthermore, it is crucial to conduct regular keyword research to ensure that we are targeting the right keywords and phrases. The search behavior of users is constantly changing, and what may have been a popular keyword last month might not be as relevant anymore. By staying on top of keyword trends and adapting our content to match the evolving search queries of our target audience, we can ensure that our website remains visible and competitive in search engine results.

In addition to keeping ourselves updated, it is equally important to monitor our competitors and learn from their successes and failures. By analyzing their SEO strategies, we can gain insights into what works and what doesn't in our industry. This can help us identify new opportunities, find innovative ways to stand out from the crowd, and adjust our own SEO efforts accordingly.

Continuous improvement and adaptation in SEO also entail the use of analytics and data to make informed decisions. By leveraging tools such as Google Analytics or SEO software, we can gain valuable insights into the performance of our website, track user behavior, and identify areas for improvement. By analyzing this data, we can identify patterns, trends, and opportunities that we can capitalize on to drive ongoing success.

In conclusion, embracing a culture of continuous improvement and adaptation in our SEO efforts is paramount to dominating search engines and staying ahead of the competition. By constantly testing and optimizing our SEO tactics, staying updated with industry changes, and leveraging analytics and data, we can drive ongoing success and maintain a competitive edge. In this dynamic and ever-evolving field, it is not enough to rely on past successes; instead, we must constantly strive to improve, adapt to change, and embrace new strategies to stay ahead of the curve. So, let us embark on this journey of continuous improvement and adaptation together, and unlock the true potential of our SEO endeavors.

AKRAM ABBASI

What's New in the Second Edition (2026 Update)

This second edition adds updates based on how SEO works in 2026.

New points added in this version:

Programmatic SEO for scalable keyword targeting

Automation + AI usage with quality control

Focus on long-tail coverage and structured templates

Safe scaling practices to avoid low-quality mass pages

8

SEO for AI Overviews, AI Mode & Answer Engines (2026 Edition)

M y dear reader,
welcome to a moment in SEO history where the rules are not merely changing — they are being rewritten.

For years, search engine optimization was about ranking links on a page. Then it became about user intent, mobile experience, and quality content. Today, as we step into 2026, SEO enters a new era: the era of AI-driven answers.

Search engines no longer wait for users to click.
They summarize.
They explain.
They guide.

And they do this through AI Overviews, AI Mode, and other answer-engine experiences.

If your content is not prepared for this shift, it risks becoming invisible — even if it ranks well. But if you understand how this system works, your content can become the source AI relies on.

So buckle up, my dear reader. Let us explore how SEO works when the search engine itself becomes the answer.

8.1 The Evolution From Search Engine To Answer Engine

Traditional search engines worked like libraries. They showed you a list of books and asked you to choose. AI-driven search works like a teacher. It reads many sources and then explains the topic to the user.

This change has three major consequences:

Fewer clicks, more summaries

More trust placed on a small number of sources

Greater importance of clarity, authority, and structure

AI Overviews and AI Mode do not invent information. They select information. Your job as an SEO professional is to ensure your content is selectable.

8.2 Understanding Ai Overviews And Ai Mode

AI Overviews appear directly on the search results page. They summarize answers using information from multiple web sources and may include citations.

Key characteristics:

Appear above traditional results

Focus on concise explanations

Prefer clear, structured, factual content

Cite sources that demonstrate trust and relevance

AI Mode

AI Mode allows users to ask complex or multi-step questions. The system responds conversationally, pulling insights from authoritative pages and encouraging deeper exploration.

In both cases, AI systems evaluate:

Clarity of explanation

Topical relevance

Entity understanding

Trustworthiness of the source

Ranking alone is no longer enough.

8.3 How Ai Chooses Content To Display

AI systems do not "think" like humans, but they evaluate content using advanced signals. To be chosen, your page must answer three silent questions:

Is this content easy to understand?

Is this source trustworthy?

Does this content clearly answer the user's question?

Let us break this down practically.

Clarity Wins

AI favors content that:

Defines concepts clearly

Uses simple language

Avoids unnecessary fluff

Answers questions early

Structure Matters

Well-structured content is easier for AI to extract:

Clear H2 and H3 headings

Bullet points and numbered steps

Short paragraphs

Dedicated answer sections

Trust Is Non-Negotiable

AI systems strongly prefer content that shows:

Author identity

Expertise or experience

Updated information

References or supporting data

8.4 Writing Content That Ai Can Use

This is where many websites fail. They write for ranking, not for explanation.

To succeed in AI-driven search, you must do both.

Step 1: Answer First, Explain Second

Begin important pages with a direct answer. Do not hide it halfway down the page.

Example structure:

Short definition or summary

Followed by detailed explanation

Then examples, steps, or comparisons

Step 2: Create "AI-Friendly Answer Blocks"

Include small, focused sections such as:

"Quick Answer"

"Key Takeaways"

"Step-by-Step Process"

"Common Mistakes"

These sections make your content easy to quote and summarize.

Step 3: Reduce Ambiguity

Avoid vague statements. Be specific.
Instead of:

"SEO is important for businesses."

Use:

"SEO helps businesses increase organic visibility, reduce paid advertising costs, and attract users with high purchase intent."

Specificity builds confidence — and AI prefers confidence.

8.5 The Role Of Entities And Context

AI does not just read words; it identifies entities and relationships.

You should clearly communicate:

Who you are

What your website represents

What topics you are authoritative in

How concepts relate to each other

Use:

Clear "About" pages

Consistent author names

Structured data where appropriate

Internal links that show topic relationships

This helps AI understand context, not just content.

8.6 Visibility Without Clicks: A New Seo Reality

One uncomfortable truth of AI search is this: Sometimes users get answers without visiting your site.

This does not mean SEO is dead. It means visibility has expanded beyond traffic.

New success indicators include:

Being cited as a source

Brand name appearing in AI answers

Increased branded searches later

Users returning directly to your site

Assisted conversions

SEO in 2026 is not only about immediate clicks — it is about long-term influence.

8.7 Optimizing For Control And Protection

Not all content should be summarized freely. In some cases, you may want to:

Limit preview length

Protect premium content

Encourage clicks for deeper value

Search engines provide mechanisms to control how content is previewed. Use them wisely to balance exposure and protection.

The goal is not to block AI — the goal is to guide it.

8.8 Common Mistakes To Avoid

Many websites fail in AI-driven SEO because they:

Over-optimize for keywords

Publish thin AI-generated content

Lack clear authorship

Ignore updates and freshness

Write for algorithms instead of humans

Remember this rule:

If a human finds your content confusing, AI will too.

8.9 Preparing For The Future Of

Answer Engines

AI search will continue to evolve. Voice assistants, multimodal search, and personalized answers are becoming normal.

To stay ahead:

Focus on explanation, not manipulation

Build authority, not shortcuts

Create content that teaches

Update important pages regularly

Think like a publisher, not a trickster

Conclusion

My dear reader,
in the age of AI Overviews and answer engines, SEO is no longer about shouting the loudest. It is about being the clearest, the most trustworthy, and the most helpful.

If your content can explain a topic better than anyone else, AI will notice.

If your site demonstrates experience and credibility, AI will trust it.

And if your brand becomes a reliable source, AI will return to it again and again.

This is not the end of SEO.
This is its next evolution.

And those who adapt will not just rank —
they will be remembered.

9

ENTITY SEO & KNOWLEDGE GRAPH OPTIMIZATION

My dear reader, up to this point in your SEO journey, you have learned how search engines read words, match queries, and reward relevance. But now, we step into a deeper and more intelligent layer of search —one where Google no longer thinks only in keywords, but in entities.

Welcome to the era where search engines do not ask "What words are on this page?"
They ask "What is this page about, who is behind it, and how is it connected to the world?"

This chapter will help you understand Entity SEO and how to align your website with the Knowledge Graph, the system that powers understanding, trust, and recommendations in modern search.

What Is An Entity In Seo?

An entity is a clearly defined "thing" that exists independently and can be uniquely identified.

Examples of entities include:

A person (author, expert, founder)

A brand or company

A place or location

A product or service

A concept or topic

Unlike keywords, entities are not just text strings. They are objects with meaning and relationships.

For example:

"Apple" as a fruit

"Apple" as a company

"Apple iPhone" as a product

Search engines use entities to remove confusion and improve accuracy. When Google understands you as an entity, it no longer guesses—it recognizes.

Why Entity SEO Matters?

Search engines now rely heavily on entity-based understanding because:

AI systems need clear, structured meaning

Ambiguous keywords are unreliable

Trust must be measured beyond content alone

Entity SEO helps search engines:

Understand who you are

Know what you specialize in

Connect your content to related topics

Decide whether you are a reliable source

In simple words:

Keywords help you appear.
Entities help you be trusted and recommended.

Understanding the Knowledge Graph

The Knowledge Graph is Google's database of entities and the relationships between them.

It connects:

people ↔ companies

brands ↔ services

topics ↔ subtopics

authors ↔ expertise

When your website is aligned with the Knowledge Graph:

Your brand becomes recognizable

Your content gains contextual strength

Your pages support each other naturally

You may already see this in action when:

Google shows a knowledge panel

A brand name triggers rich results

An author is associated with a topic

These are not accidents. They are entity signals.

Building Your Core Website Entities

Every serious website should clearly define its core entities.

1. Brand Entity

Your brand must be unambiguous:

consistent name

clear description

same logo, colors, and messaging everywhere

Create a strong About Us page that explains:

who you are

what you do

who you help

when you were founded

This page is not for marketing only—it is for understanding.

2. Author / Expert Entity

Search engines want to know who is speaking.

Every important article should be tied to:

a real author

with a bio

with experience and credibility

Your author page should include:

full name

role or expertise

professional background

links to social or professional profiles

This strengthens trust and supports E-E-A-T principles already discussed earlier in your book.

3. Service / Topic Entities

Each major service or topic should have:

one strong "entity page"

clearly defined scope

supporting articles linked to it

Avoid scattering the same topic across many weak pages.
Instead, create one authoritative hub and connect everything else to it.

Entity-Based Content Structure

Entity SEO requires a shift in how you organize content.

From isolated posts → to topic ecosystems

Instead of writing random articles, build:

a pillar page for the main entity

multiple supporting pages

strong internal links that explain relationships

Example:

Main entity: Technical SEO

Supporting entities:

crawl budget

site speed

schema

indexing

JavaScript SEO

This structure teaches search engines how ideas relate, not just what keywords exist.

Structured Data as an Entity Translator

Structured data (schema) helps search engines confirm what they already suspect.

Schema does not guarantee rankings, but it:

reduces ambiguity

reinforces entity definitions

connects your site to known entity types

Important schemas for Entity SEO include:

Organization

Person

Article

Product

LocalBusiness

Use schema honestly and accurately.
Never mark up something that is not real.

Remember:

Schema clarifies meaning—it does not create it.

Consistency: The Hidden Power of Entity SEO

Entities thrive on consistency.

Your brand, author, and business details should be:

identical on your website

consistent across social profiles

matching business listings

aligned with citations and mentions

Even small differences can weaken entity recognition:

name variations

address mismatches

conflicting descriptions

Consistency builds confidence.
Confidence builds trust.
Trust builds visibility.

Brand Mentions and Entity Reinforcement

Links are powerful, but mentions also matter.

When other websites mention:

your brand name

your author name

your company or product

Search engines treat these as entity reinforcement signals, even without a clickable link.

This is why:

PR

citations

interviews

references

are all part of modern SEO—not just backlinks.

Entity SEO and AI Search

AI-driven search systems rely heavily on entity understanding.

When your entity is strong:

AI systems can summarize you correctly

your content is easier to cite

your expertise is easier to trust

Weak entities are ignored.

Strong entities are referenced.

This is why Entity SEO directly supports:

Ai Overviews

knowledge-based answers

brand-driven visibility

Common Entity SEO Mistakes

Avoid these errors:

anonymous content with no author

weak or missing About pages

inconsistent brand information

multiple pages competing for the same entity

using schema without clear real-world signals

Entity SEO is not a trick—it is alignment with reality.

Conclusion

My dear reader, Entity SEO is not about gaming algorithms.
It is about being understood.

In a world where search engines think more like humans, clarity beats cleverness, structure beats chaos, and identity beats repetition.

When search engines know who you are,
understand what you represent,
and trust how you connect ideas,

you no longer chase rankings—
rankings begin to follow you.

10

Programmatic SEO & Scalable Automation

P rogrammatic SEO is used when you want to target hundreds or thousands of similar keywords using a structured approach.

It is not about creating low-quality pages.
It is about creating useful pages at scale.

10.1 What Is Programmatic Seo

Programmatic SEO means creating many SEO pages using:

templates

structured data

automation

Instead of writing each page manually, pages are generated based on data.

Each page targets a specific long-tail keyword.

10.2 When Programmatic Seo Is Useful

Programmatic SEO works best when:

keywords follow a clear pattern

content can be structured

data is available

Common examples:

service + city pages

product comparison pages

location-based listings

software comparisons

directories and catalogs

10.3 Core Elements Of Programmatic Seo

To succeed, these elements are required:

1. Data Source

Pages must be based on real data such as:

product lists

services

locations

prices

features

Without real data, pages become thin and useless.

2. Page Template

Each page should include:

page title

short introduction

main content sections

Faqs

internal links

Templates must be helpful, not empty.

3. Automation

Automation can be done using:

CMS templates

spreadsheets

databases

APIs

AI tools (with control)

Automation should always be reviewed before publishing.

10.4 Programmatic Seo And Ai Content

AI can help in programmatic SEO, but it must be used carefully.

AI can be used to:

explain data

write short descriptions

generate FAQs

AI should not be used to:

publish thousands of identical pages

generate content without data

skip human review

Quality control is mandatory.

10.5 Common Programmatic Seo Mistakes

Avoid these mistakes:

publishing thin pages

indexing all pages without testing

scaling too fast

duplicate content across pages

poor internal linking

These mistakes can cause:

poor rankings

deindexing

penalties

10.6 Best Practices For Safe Scaling

Follow these steps:

Create a small number of pages first

Check indexing and rankings

Improve the template

Fix weak content

Scale gradually

Always test before scaling.

10.7 Programmatic Seo And Technical Seo

Programmatic pages require:

fast loading speed

clean URLs

proper internal links

canonical tags

index/noindex control

Technical issues can affect thousands of pages at once.

10.8 Measuring Programmatic Seo Success

Track:

indexed pages

impressions

long-tail keyword growth

internal link depth

conversions

Do not focus only on traffic.
Focus on coverage and consistency.

Conclusion

Programmatic SEO is a powerful strategy when used correctly.

It allows you to:

scale content

target long-tail searches

build topical authority

But without quality control, it can damage your website.

Use automation wisely.
Scale value, not just pages.

SEO SUCCESS CRUCIAL ASPECT OF ANY DIGITAL MARKETING STRATEGY

1. Keyword Ranking and Visibility:
2. Organic Traffic Growth:
3. Click-Through Rate (CTR):
4. Bounce Rate and Dwell Time:
5. Conversion Rate:
6. Return on Investment (ROI):
7. Quality and Relevance of Traffic:
8. Mobile and Local SEO Metrics:
9. User Engagement Metrics:

10. **Competitive Analysis**:

11. **Content Performance**:

12. **Technical SEO Health**:

13. **User Experience (UX)**:

14. **Long-Term Trends and Patterns**:

15. **Feedback and User Surveys**: